HOW TO BECOME A BETTER NEGOTIATOR

SECOND EDITION

HOW TO BECOME A BETTER NEGOTIATOR

SECOND EDITION

Richard A. Luecke
James G. Patterson

AMACOM

AMER   N

New York • Atlanta • Brussels • Chicago • Mexico City • San Francisco
Shanghai • Tokyo • Toronto • Washington, D.C.

Special discounts on bulk quantities of AMACOM books
are available to corporations, professional associations,
and other organizations. For details, contact Special
Sales Department, AMACOM, a division of American
Management Association, 1601 Broadway, New York,
NY 10019.
Tel: 212-903-8316. Fax: 212-903-8083.
E-mail: specialsls@amanet.org
Website: www.amacombooks.org/go/specialsales
To view all AMACOM titles go to:
www.amacombooks.org

This publication is designed to provide accurate and
authoritative information in regard to the subject matter
covered. It is sold with the understanding that the publisher is
not engaged in rendering legal, accounting, or other
professional service. If legal advice or other expert assistance
is required, the services of a competent professional person
should be sought.

Library of Congress Cataloging-in-Publication Data

Luecke, Richard A.
    How to become a better negotiator / Richard A. Luecke, James G. Patterson.
— 2nd ed.
        p.   cm.
    Rev. ed. of: How to become a better negotiator / James G. Patterson. 1996.
    Includes bibliographical references and index.
    ISBN 978-0-8144-0047-0 (pbk.)
    1. Negotiation in business.   I. Patterson, James G.   II. Patterson, James G.
How to become a better negotiator.   III. Title.

HD58.6.L83   2008
658.4'052—dc22   2007033525

Printing number

10   9   8   7   6   5   4   3   2   1

CONTENTS

PREFACE

N egotiations are a means of resolving differences between people when imposed settlements are not possible. And because so much of our work and personal lives involve resolving differences, the ability to negotiate effectively is an essential life skill. Almost everything we do involves some kind of negotiation. If you think about it, you'll realize that you negotiate all the time, every day. You negotiated to get your new job and a raise. You negotiated with coworkers about where to hold your last meeting. You negotiated with your spouse and other loved ones about where to take a vacation.

When we buy and sell things, sell ideas, and solve problems that involve others, negotiation gets us what we want. Negotiation is a way to get one's fair share, whether it's selling a proposal to your boss, settling a labor dispute, buying real estate, or getting that new car.

Most Americans are uncomfortable with negotiations (remember the last time you bought a new car?). This may be the consequence of bad experiences or of feeling unprepared to do them well. Ours, unlike some others in the world, is a haggle-free culture. And most Americans seem to prefer it that way. As evidence, consider the customer response to Saturn Corporation's introduction of its no-haggle sales policy: Here's the car, here's the price. People loved it.

You can learn to be a good negotiator if:

- You know what you want and what you are willing to give up.

- You know (or have a good idea) what the other side wants and what it is willing to give up.

- You come to the table with a "how can we both win" attitude.

- You are skilled in problem solving, listening, basic conflict management, and the uses of tactics and strategies in negotiating.

This book contains nine chapters, each building upon those preceding.

Chapter 1, "Win-Lose or Win-Win," describes the two basic types of negotiations. This book advocates for win-win deals in which each party is satisfied and better off with the result. However, we recognize that not everyone you meet will want to play this game, so the chapter will explain the characteristics of both types.

Chapter 2 describes three important concepts you'll need to prepare for your negotiating experience: alternatives to a negotiated deal, reserve price, and area of potential agreement. Chapter 3, "Communication Styles," which describes the main communications styles, helps you discover your dominant style and gives you tips on how to adapt your style to be more effective with people who use very different styles. Chapter 4 is on listening—an important skill for every negotiator. Most of us assume that we know how to listen. After all, we have two ears, don't we? You will learn that listening is not the same as hearing, and that it takes a lot more to listen effectively than simply to hear. You'll learn whether or not you are a good listener and how you can be a better listener to maximize your negotiating results. Chapter 5, "Managing Conflict," will help you to learn your preferred style of handling conflict situations, how to use conflict resolution styles effectively, and how to use a multistep problem-solving method to handle conflict in negotiations.

In the push and pull of negotiations, <u>assertiveness</u> matters. Whether you're dealing with your spouse about who will do which household chores or representing your department in an interdepartmental meeting, assertiveness is important. Chapter 6 will help you take your own measure of assertiveness and explains various strategies to handle difficult people and situations.

The final three chapters of the book get down to the brass tacks of negotiating. They describe how you go about preparing (Chapter 7), and offer strategies (Chapter 8) such as anchoring, counteranchoring, and dealing with hostile or overbearing opponents. Chapter 9 wraps things up with a description of common negotiating ploys you're bound to encounter—and how to deal with them, as well as typical negotiating mistakes that people make and how you can avoid them. That chapter ends with timely guidance on how to negotiate across national and cultural boarders.

Negotiation is a uniquely human and humane activity. It provides nations, organizations, and individuals with opportunities to reduce conflict and to settle differences in mutually beneficial ways. Thus, mastering the art and practice of negotiation will help you improve your life, your business, and the world around you.

Good luck with your next negotiation!

HOW TO BECOME A BETTER NEGOTIATOR

SECOND EDITION

CHAPTER 1

WIN-LOSE OR WIN-WIN

G enerally, negotiations fall into one of two types: win-lose or win-win. It's important to understand the difference between these because each requires a different attitude and set of tactics.

WIN-LOSE

In a win-lose negotiation, the matter at stake involves a fixed value, and each party aims to get as much of that value as possible. Anything gained by one party is achieved at the expense of the other, which is why a win-lose situation is also known as a "zero-sum game." People often use the example of a pie in explaining a win-lose situation. Whatever you manage to carve out of that pie for yourself reduces the amount of pie that the other person will get— and vice versa. So your job in this game is to get as big a slice as you possibly can (Figure 1–1).

Win-lose situations are common in these circumstances:

FIGURE 1-1 THE WIN-LOSE NEGOTIATION

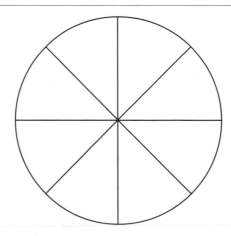

- Price is all that matters.
- There is no expectation of a continuing relationship with the other side.
- One side has greater bargaining power than the other.

For example, think about that new car you bought last year. Having done your homework, you knew exactly which model you wanted, your color preferences, and the options that appealed to you. A little research told you what price the different dealers were asking for that model and, thanks to some online research, you knew what those dealers paid for that model (dealer invoice price) and the different options. Another online search gave you a good idea what you might expect for a trade-in of your old car.

Chances are that every dealer visit you made included some haggling about price. When the objective of the negotiation is a commodity-like product, such as a particular car model, price is generally the main issue. If Dealers A, B, C, and D each had the car you wanted, there wasn't much besides price to negotiate about.

Your relationship with the car salesperson and the dealer didn't matter either. It was clear to you that the salesperson and his boss were trying to get as much out of the deal as possible—charging as much as they could for the car, trying to "upsell" you on expensive options you didn't want or need ("For only $700, we can protect your investment by installing the patented *Gotcha!* theft-deterrent system"), and lowballing the value of your trade-in ("Our mechanic has found lots of problems with your car"). So you weren't planning to do business with these people again. You were after the car.

In win-lose deals, relationships don't matter.

Simply put, your job was to come away with the greatest possible value—a win-lose proposition—and the salesperson was trying to do the same.

Participants in win-lose negotiations perceive a *fixed* amount of value. As they carve up the value "pie" each tries to carve out as big a piece as possible for himself. And every gain by one party represents a one-to-one loss to the other.

WIN-WIN

Very few negotiations involve a fixed value or a commodity product. There's generally at least one or more ways that the parties can alter the value of the deal or product or service at the heart of their negotiations—in effect, enlarging the pie. In these situations, price is only one of several issues that matter. The quality of the product or service, the reliability of the other party, or the importance of one's relationship with the other party may be just as important as price.

In win-win deals, relationships often matter.

Consider a negotiation between MakeCo—a manufacturer—and one of its long-term suppliers, WidgetWorks. MakeCo is trying to negotiate a purchase agreement for 10,000 widgets built to its specifications for $5 apiece, to be delivered in lots of 1,000 units as needed. WidgetWorks wants to keep MakeCo's business but needs a higher price—say $5.50—to earn an acceptable profit for itself and **its** shareholders. Getting this higher price will be difficult since several other competitors are asking for less.

On the surface, this might be just another win-lose situation, with each trying to get the best price. But it's possible that MakeCo and WidgetWorks have a relationship that's worth more than price per widget. For example, MakeCo appreciates and values Widget-Works's reliability. When WidgetWorks says, "We will have 2,000 units at your receiving dock by Friday morning," MakeCo's production planners know from experience that they can rely on those units being there when they need them. "Other vendors are quoting a lower price," says MakeCo's purchasing manager, "but their reliability hasn't been demonstrated. Who knows? They might be out of business in six months, leaving us in a real jam."

Further, the two companies—buyer and supplier—have been working together so long that their engineers are accustomed to collaborating on the design of new widgets and the materials used to make them.

For its part, WidgetWorks has every reason to want MakeCo to succeed in its business. "They've been a valued customer for over 12 years now," says WidgetWorks's CEO. "When they win, we win." And so, as they negotiate, each company is motivated to reach an agreement that will satisfy the interests of both parties.

In some cases it costs little or nothing to satisfy the interests of the other party, even as you do well for yourself. This is achieved by *creating value through trades*—that is, giving up something that is of little value to you, but that the other party values highly. Consider this example:

When Boston Brewing Company, maker of Samuel Adams beer, first went into business, it didn't have enough orders to financially justify a multimillion-dollar, state-of-the-art plant. Meanwhile, a brewery in Pennsylvania found that it had more production capacity than it could use; part of its costly plant was idle.

These two companies saw an opportunity to create value

through trade. For the Pennsylvania brewery, every case of Samuel Adams beer it bottled using that company's unique recipe would produce revenue it could use to cover the fixed costs of its plant. As long as it charged enough to cover the added cost of labor and ingredients (variable costs), it would be money ahead. For Boston Brewing Company, contracting production to the Pennsylvania facility would eliminate the need to build a multimillion-dollar plant of its own. At the same time, it knew that it would get consistently high quality for its customers.

So the two companies struck a deal. The Boston company sent its brewmeister to Pennsylvania, where he supervised production of Samuel Adams beer. The price it paid for each case was far less than the cost of producing beer in its own facility. The brewery was equally pleased with the deal; its idle capacity was now making money.

The deal struck by these two companies produced a win-win.

WHAT ABOUT YOU?

Can you think of win-win examples from your own experience? Perhaps you've asked your boss for a raise. "I don't have the money in my budget for a raise," she says, "but I can offer you something more valuable. I can assign you to a project that will broaden your experience and skills, making you more promotable in the future." You will gain something of value in this trade at no cost to your boss. A win-win.

Be Creative—Look for Interests

Not every win-lose situation can be turned into a negotiation in which both parties can come out ahead. However, it is often possible to do that if you apply a little creativity. For instance, you'd think that buying a house would be a win-lose situation. As a buyer, every dollar you manage to trim from the seller's price is a gain for you and a loss to her. But if you think creatively, you may find opportunities to create value through trade. Consider this example:

> The seller of a house you want to buy is asking $450,000. This seller obviously values money (as do you), but ask yourself, *Is there something I could painlessly trade off in return for a lower price?* A bit of dialogue with the seller may reveal that she is also concerned with the *timing* of the sale. You may find, for instance, that because of a job transfer to another city she wants to purchase a new home in November. Her plans would be disrupted if she could not unload her house and buy the new one at the same time.
>
> And so your creative side tells you, *If I were to buy her house in, say, September, she'd have to store all of her furniture and rent an apartment for two months—both major hassles.* You can create a trade this seller will value if you say, "My schedule is flexible. I can accommodate your situation and conclude the sale in November if you are willing to come down a bit on the price." She may figure that the hassle of storing her furniture for two months—and two months of apartment rent—is worth $5,000. And so, in horse-trading fashion, she may say, "Great! If we can close the sale in November, I'll reduce the price to $445,000."

Thus, by understanding the interests of the other side—and by applying a bit of creativity—you will have created a situation in which both parties are better off. Win, win! These situations emerge from an understanding of the other side's interests. We'll return later to the importance of understanding the interests of the participating negotiators—both yours and those of others. The better you understand those interests, the more effective you'll be as a negotiator.

LOSE-LOSE

Although most negotiations can be described as win-lose or win-win, some result in a "lose" for all parties. In this game, both sides lose something in the negotiations. The best example of a lose-lose game is a compromise in which the total value of the deal is diminished. We've always been taught that compromise is a good thing. However, a series of compromises can leave both sides with far less than they needed in the first place. One example of a lose-lose game is that of a union that makes unreasonable demands and winds up forcing a company to close. In this case, both the company and union members are losers.

CHAPTER REVIEW

Test what you've learned so far with this open-book review quiz.

1. Explain the characteristics of a win-lose negotiation.

_____

_____

2. How would you describe the value of relationships in win-lose deals?

_____

_____

3. Describe a win-win negotiation from your own experience.

_____

_____

4. What is meant by "creating value through trade?"

_____

_____

CHAPTER 2

THREE INDISPENSABLE CONCEPTS

S uccessful negotiating is based on a sound conceptual foundation. This chapter introduces three indispensable negotiating concepts and explains how you can use them to good effect. Those concepts are:

1. Alternatives

2. Reserve price

3. Area of potential agreement

ALTERNATIVES

The first important concept at the negotiator's disposal is one or more practical alternatives to the deal currently on the table. Alternatives make it possible for a negotiator to say, "If this negotiation fails to produce what I need, I can always do _____." Consider this simple example:

You are selling your house and already have an offer from a qualified buyer for $400,000. A second potential buyer has come into the picture, this one offering $375,000. You counter that second offer, asking for $449,000. As you negotiate with this second buyer, you know that you have someone ready to pay you $400,000 for the house.

In effect, alternatives give the negotiator a credible walk-away opportunity. In theory at least, the negotiator shouldn't accept any deal that is less attractive than his or her most attractive alternative.

Roger Fisher and William Ury introduced this concept, which they call Best Alternative to a Negotiated Agreement, or BATNA, in their popular book, *Getting to Yes.* Every negotiator should have a BATNA in his or her hip pocket. To appreciate its value, consider a more complex example, the case of an ambitious young manager, Helen, who is trying to negotiate an expanded role with her Chicago-based employer. She introduced this matter to her boss months ago, and they are now in serious negotiations.

Helen has proposed that the company move her from Chicago to Boston, where she will create a new sales district, with herself as manager. Once there, she will recruit a regional sales force, develop a new customer base for the company, and identify potential sales targets. As part of her proposal, the company will pay for Helen's move, name her manager of its Northeastern sales district, and provide a salary and incentives commensurate with her larger responsibilities.

Helen knows that tough negotiations lie ahead. Opening a new operation in Boston will involve substantial start-up costs and business risks. But she sees the move as a great opportunity—both for the company and for her career.

Before entering into discussions with her boss and the company's executive team, Helen does her homework.

She develops a plan for implementing her proposition, with cost and revenue estimates. Just as important, she thinks about alternatives if the company turns her down:

- Alternative 1: Helen can keep her current job, which is fine for now but not something she wants to do much longer. "I plan to move up or move out within one year," she tells herself.

- Alternative 2: The manager of the Southwestern sales district is planning to retire; he has told Helen in confidence that he will support her selection as his replacement.

- Alternative 3: Helen has had informal discussions with a rival company, which has been trying to recruit her for the past year. It would put her on the fast track to a higher-level job.

Always have an alternative to the deal.

In this scenario, Helen has some aces—that is, some alternatives—up her sleeve. If the company stonewalls her plan, or will only accept a weak version of it, she doesn't have to accept its offer. She can walk away knowing that she has attractive alternatives. Assuming that the company values her as an up-and-coming employee, Helen might even leak some information about Alternative 3, the overtures she's received from a rival company. The thought of losing her talents to a competitor might induce the company to give Helen what she wants.

Helen can negotiate from a position of strength and confidence because she has alternatives. She knows when she can walk away from an offer. Compare her savvy use of alternatives to the person who enters a negotiation with *no* alternatives. That person has no bargaining chips, no leverage, and no basis for confidence. Unless he can bluff his way to a good outcome, he is doomed to accept whatever deal the other side offers.

. . . .

NEGOTIATING TIP: IMPROVE YOUR BEST ALTERNATIVE BEFORE GETTING INTO SERIOUS NEGOTIATIONS.

A local business person has called to say, "I'd like to buy your company for $1 million." Your current best alternative is to keep running your company as it is. You might improve that alternative by asking a business broker to solicit bids from other buyers. Those other bids may produce a more valuable alternative—say, a purchase offer of $1.25 million.

. . . .

RESERVE PRICE

Have you ever bought or sold anything on eBay, the online auction site? If you have, you've encountered the term *reserve price*, which is the lowest price the seller will accept for an item—it is the dollar amount below which the seller will walk away from any deal (or the amount above which the bidder will not pay). Naturally, that price is not disclosed to bidders. Every negotiator should determine his or her reserve price *in advance* of any negotiation. Consider this example:

> Oscar and Janis are listing their business for sale with a business broker. As part of their discussions with the broker, they say, "Based on your assessment of the market and the appraised value of our business, we'd like you to list it at $795,000. However, just between you and us, we'll entertain offers down to $725,000. That's our reserve price; we are unwilling to sell below that amount."

Your reserve price is your *walk-away* price.

The wise negotiator determines reserve price only after careful thought. Consider Oscar and Janis. They did not pull the number

$725,000 out of a hat! Instead, that number resulted from a professional appraiser's valuation of their business and the amount that the partners determined necessary to make the deal worthwhile to them. "If we can't get at least $725,000," Janis told Oscar, "we won't have enough money to retire in the style we'd like. We'd be better off keeping and running the business." Naturally, they will not disclose their reserve price to the other side.

Sellers aren't the only ones who should know their reserve price; buyers should also have one in mind as they enter a negotiation. For example, if you are shopping for a house, you should have a dollar amount *above which* you will not pay. That's your *walk-away* point.

- -

NEGOTIATING TIP: TRY TO LEARN THE OTHER SIDE'S RESERVE PRICE WITHOUT REVEALING YOUR OWN.

If you can learn the other side's reserve price—or approximate it—you'll know how hard you can push without forcing that person to walk away.

- -

AREA OF AGREEMENT

The notion of a reserve price sets up the next negotiating tool: the *area of agreement,* or the price range within which a deal is possible that will satisfy both parties. To understand this concept, let's return to the case of our business partners, Oscar and Janis. As sellers, their reserve price is $725,000. Any offer less than that will make them walk away. Now let's suppose that George, a potential buyer, comes along. He likes their little enterprise and would pay up to $750,000 for it—no more. That's George's reserve price.

Figure 2–1 describes the area of agreement in this particular case. Naturally, George will try to get the business for less than $750,000, and Oscar and Janis will attempt to get more than their $725,000 reserve price. However, there is room for negotiating a

FIGURE 2-1 AREA OF AGREEMENT

Oscar & Janis's reserve price	George's reserve price
$725,000 ◄----------- Area of Agreement -----------►	$750,000

deal satisfactory to both sides within this range. We can easily imagine that buyer and seller would haggle, each would give some ground, and they'd strike a deal somewhere between the high and low figure.

Now, suppose that the figures were reversed, that George wouldn't pay more than $725,000 and the sellers would not take less than $750,000 for their business. In that case, there would be *no area of potential agreement*. Barring some change in reserve prices or other factors, there would be no possibility for a negotiated deal between these parties based on price. Each side would walk away.

. . . .

Alternatives. Reserve price. Area of agreement. These are concepts that you should understand as a negotiator. We'll explain some of their practical applications in later chapters.

CHAPTER REVIEW

Check your understanding of negotiating concepts by taking this open-book review test.

1. How can a best alternative to a negotiated deal help you when dealing with the other side?

_____

_____

2. Think about your most recent negotiation. Did you have a best alternative in mind? How could you have strengthened your best alternative in that case?

_____

_____

3. Explain the reserve price concept.

_____

_____

4. What do you call the area between the buyer's reserve price and the seller's reserve price? What does it make possible?

_____

_____

CHAPTER 3

COMMUNICATION STYLES

E ffective negotiators are good communicators. Good communicators communicate in a style that is appropriate for the situation and for the people with whom they are dealing. The
wrong style may impede the progress of a negotiation. For example, demanding or threatening is an inappropriate style when the
purpose of the negotiation is to forge a willing and collaborative
relationship between parties.

The late President Ronald Reagan—billed by many as the Great
Communicator—surely understood the importance of using the
right style. In one memorable case, Reagan was debating a member
of the U.S. Senate on the issue of taxation before a general television audience. Reagan wanted to reduce taxes on citizens—those
same citizens who made up the audience. The senator wanted to
explain why high taxes were necessary. The senator cited statistics
and budgets; he recited the different tax rates for different income
groups, other minutiae of the nation's mind-boggling tax code, and
prattled on and on for many minutes. When Reagan's time to speak
arrived, he did the opposite. His message was short, simple, and

devastating to his opponent: "I don't doubt the details you've described, Senator, but your conclusions are wrong. When America's working people look at their pay stubs, they want to know one thing: 'Why is so little of this paycheck going to me and so much going to the government?'" Reagan was communicating in a style that made sense to his listeners while the senator was talking the talk of the policy wonks back in Washington.

Good negotiators try to do what Reagan did in that example: Instead of trying to negotiate with everyone the same way, they first try to understand which style will be most effective, then reach people in a way in which they want to be reached.

THE FOUR COMMUNICATION STYLES

The notion of different styles is not simply a theory. A body of research supports the existence of individual differences in styles of learning and communicating. In the 1920s, for example, the Swiss psychoanalyst Carl Jung asserted that people develop and use one dominant behavior style. Other researchers, like the American psychologist Paul Mot, have suggested that people behave, communicate, and learn according to one of four styles: Listener, Creator, Doer, and Thinker. Let's take a closer look at those styles, each of which can help us become better negotiators.

Style I: Listeners

Listeners are people oriented. They believe that there is more than one method for producing the same results. While they demand a voice in decisions that affect them, they can be slow decision makers. They want to talk about the issues and get to know you as a person. They place a high premium on relationships. Because of this, they are often good mediators and team builders. But they just can't say no. Everybody's priorities become their priorities. Perhaps because of this, they are easily sidetracked. They seek security in their job and are not big risk takers. And, they are the last people (along with Thinkers) to volunteer to make a presentation!

Are you a Listener? If you are, you can improve your effectiveness by being more assertive, forcing yourself to focus less on relationships and more on tasks and outcomes, and learning to make observations based on fact, not subjective judgments. In negotiations, many Listeners turn into pacifiers, always seeking to make all sides happier.

If you're not a Listener, you can negotiate successfully with them if you can identify their objectives. Listeners will then reach the objective in their own way. When given the freedom to do so, these people like to prove themselves. So be more casual and personal with them. Be relaxed, and show interest in them as people. Know that when Listeners are under stress, they are often submissive and indecisive. That may present you with an opportunity.

Listeners have the most conflict when engaging with Doers, their polar opposites.

Style II: Creators

Creators are enthusiastic and excitement-driven people. Their excitement is often contagious and persuasive. They don't mind breaking away from the negotiations and having fun. Creators can be impulsive and often make decisions on the spot. They are idea people but often fail to act on their great ideas. That is one of the negatives associated with Creators—they have a problem with follow-through. The thrill for them is the idea; they tend to lose interest during follow-through, which makes them "priority jumpers" in many cases. Creators dislike routine and enjoy fast-paced conversations. When stressed, they often try to change the subject.

There's an old saying that goes, "God invented us with two ears and one mouth for a reason—so that we'd listen more than we talk." Creators, being big talkers, should take that saying to heart. They can improve their communication with others by slowing down, containing their enthusiasm a bit, and taking the time to listen to other people and understand their interests and points of view.

If you want to communicate effectively with Creators, understand their need for their ideas to be recognized. Get them excited about a project and they will use their enthusiasm to sell others. Then be ready for a fast decision reflecting their excitement.

Creators tend to have the most conflict with Thinkers.

Style III: Doers

Doers are pragmatic, assertive, results oriented, competitive, and competent. They are no-nonsense, take-charge, get-it-done people. Like Creators, they are highly verbal. Doers tend to be excellent problem solvers, and they take the biggest risks. On the negative side, they may be arrogant and domineering, lack trust in others, exhibit short-range thinking, and act without proper planning or reflection. In their rush to get things moving they can be abrupt and dictatorial, and they may be bad listeners. They tend to be time-conscious people. Do you see that person continually glancing at a clock? It's a good bet that he or she is a Doer.

In negotiations, Doers tend to be "street fighters." They often find it hard to play "win-win" negotiating because they can be unconcerned with others' needs. They negotiate to win.

Are you a Doer? If you are, you can improve your communication by spending more time listening and allowing others to participate in negotiating sessions. Those other negotiators can get along better with Doers by getting to the point quickly. They shouldn't waste time, but be results oriented, and avoid getting bogged down with a lot of details.

Doers tend to have the greatest conflict with Listeners.

Style IV: Thinkers

Thinkers are detail-oriented people. They are slow and deliberative in making decisions ("Let's run the numbers one more time") because they are always looking for the perfect solution. Thinkers are at home with rules, regulations, and predictability. Unlike Doers, Thinkers tend to be averse to risk. Thinkers might be described as deliberative, proper, conservative, objective, and analytical; they like to weigh all of the alternatives. In the worst cases, they are subject to "paralysis through analysis." They can also be verbose, indecisive, overly serious, and rigid.

Thinkers can improve their communication with others by moving faster, showing less need for endless detail, being less rigid about following policies, taking more risks, facing conflict, and showing more personal concern for others.

If you're not a Thinker, how can you negotiate with them? One way is to demonstrate that you have thought through your position or recommendation. Remember, these are people who respect those who have done their homework. And because Thinkers are logical and analytical, adopt the tools of their trade—use charts and graphs to show the data and your line of reasoning. Allow time for them to verify your facts and reasoning. Remember, Thinkers are motivated by accuracy, logic, and data.

Thinkers tend to have the most conflict with Creators.

UNDERSTAND YOUR DOMINANT COMMUNICATION STYLE

There are no pure Creators, Thinkers, Listeners, or Doers. Each of us is a mixture of communication styles. No one style is the "right" style, or better than any of the others, nor is anyone trapped in a particular style. The important thing is to recognize your dominant style, understand its negatives, and work on containing those negatives. Also, understand the dominant styles of the people you deal with, and learn to adapt to them. Adapting to the other party's style is a way of getting on the same wavelength with that person. And once you've done that, your negotiations will go much more smoothly.

Before we move on, take a moment to think about the people with whom you currently do business on a regular basis— coworkers, customers, and people with whom you are negotiating.

Then take a look at Figure 3–1. Where would you locate those people in the 2-by-2 style matrix? Where would you locate yourself?

STYLE DIAGNOSIS

Not sure of your dominant communication style? Then take the unscientific test in Figure 3–2. Read each phrase and check the *one word* that best describes you. Then count up the check marks in each of the four columns. At the end of the quiz, you'll find the scoring key.

You should now have a good idea of your dominant style. What if you don't have a dominant style (seven or more checks in one area)? Having three or four checks in all four styles may indicate that you have an easier time than most of us communicating with all kinds of people. Those with a couple of moderate scores and one or two very low scores probably have the hardest time communicating with people who are strongest in their low-scoring (zero to two checks) areas.

FIGURE 3-1 THE FOUR COMMUNICATION STYLES

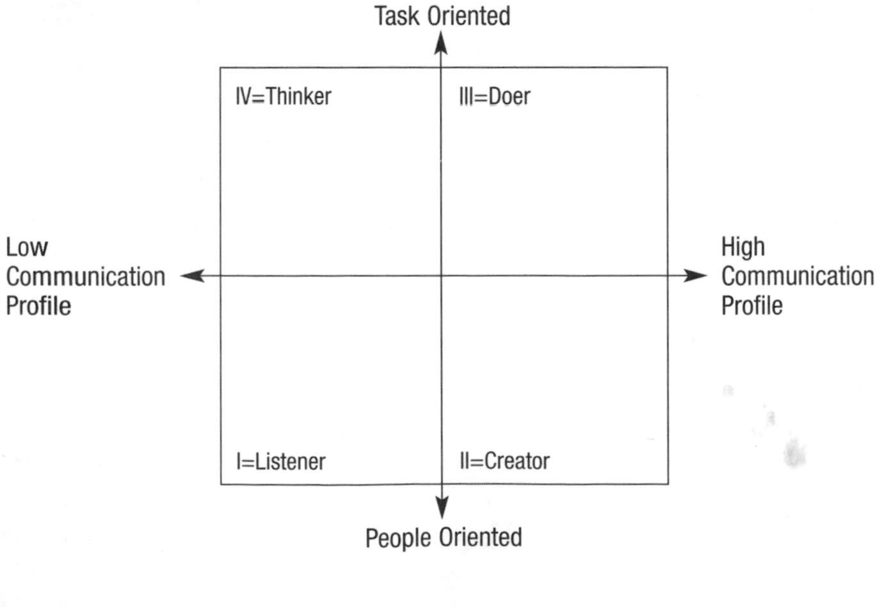

FIGURE 3-2 SELF-DIAGNOSTIC COMMUNICATION STYLE TEST

	(Listener)	*(Creator)*	*(Doer)*	*(Thinker)*
1. Your manner is basically	*accepting*	*friendly*	*controlling*	*evaluative*
2. Decision making	*slow*	*emotional*	*impulsive*	*fact based*
3. Talk about	*personal things*	*people*	*achievements*	*organization*
4. Using time	*not rushed*	*socializer*	*rushed*	*runs late*
5. Relates to others	*accepting*	*empathizer*	*commands*	*assessing*
6. Gestures	*sparse*	*open*	*impatient*	*closed*
7. Clothing preferences	*conforms*	*very stylish*	*formal*	*conservative*
8. Work pace	*steady*	*enthusiastic*	*fast*	*controlled*
9. Listening	*interested*	*distracted*	*impatient*	*selective*
10. Work area has	*keepsakes*	*pictures*	*awards*	*charts*
11. Oriented toward	*support*	*people*	*results*	*facts*
12. Basic personality	*easygoing*	*outgoing*	*dominating*	*no nonsense*
13. Communication	*low key*	*animated*	*direct*	*reserved*
14. Responsive to others	*steady*	*friendly*	*restless*	*distant*
TOTALS	*(Listener)*	*(Creator)*	*(Doer)*	*(Thinker)*

Scoring Key

7 or more = Strong preference   5–6 = Moderate preference   0–4 = Low preference

PUTTING IT TOGETHER

People naturally prefer to deal with others who share their own communication style. Problems arise when negotiators have different styles. Doers, for example, are frustrated by Listeners, who are slower to move toward conclusions or implementation of plans. Doers want Listeners to take the facts and make a decision. Listeners want Doers to go beyond the facts and care about people. Thinkers believe Creators are too flippant and easygoing. Creators, for their part, feel that Thinkers get too bogged down in details to see a higher vision.

> Negotiations between Listeners and Doers, or between Creators and Thinkers, are the hardest.

Now let's suppose that you're trying to connect with a group or an individual. You know that you can increase your chance of reaching people by tailoring your message to their particular primary style. Thus, for the primary Creator you might ask, "How do you react to the basic concepts presented here?" You can rephrase that question for a Thinker by asking, "Based on your own analysis, how are the facts I've presented relevant?" For Listeners you might ask, "How do you feel about what we've discussed?" And for the Doer, you could ask, "I'd like to move on from here; what's your reaction to my main point?"

Knowing that we don't all learn and communicate in the same way can be of great value to you. With a little practice, you'll understand people's different styles and learn to use a variety of methods to get on your listener's wavelength. This is especially important when your opponents' team shows more than one strong style.

Keep in mind that your favorite negotiating style may not be the best way to reach everybody all the time. However, adopting an alternative style that conflicts with your dominant one isn't easy. It will take a while until you get comfortable using another style, but it is worth the effort. Consciously try to reach others where *they* are, not where *you* are. If you do, you'll experience far fewer destructive conflicts and elicit more cooperation from the people with whom you are dealing.

CHAPTER REVIEW

Take the following open-book review quiz to find out what you have learned so far.

1. What are the four styles of communicating and negotiating?

_____

_____

_____

_____

2. What is your dominant style?

_____

3. What three negative communication characteristics do you need to work on?

_____

_____

_____

4. What is the communication style of the most difficult person you know?

_____

5. What can you do to improve communication with this person?

_____

_____

_____

_____

CHAPTER 4

LISTENING AS A PRIMARY NEGOTIATING SKILL

D o you remember where you were on January 28, 1986? On that day, a worldwide television audience watched in horror as the *Challenger* space shuttle blew up shortly after takeoff. A government investigation into the explosion and the deaths of the eight crew members found that pressure to go ahead with the launch had interfered with the willingness and the ability of launch officials to listen to the concerns of engineers about the safety of the spacecraft. A presidential investigative team later recommended that the National Aeronautics and Space Administration (NASA) develop plans and policies to improve communication—and listening is communication—at all levels of the organization.

WHAT IS LISTENING?

A good listener hears, interprets, evaluates, and reacts.

The *Challenger* tragedy highlights one of the biggest problems present in any large or small organization: Few people practice effective listening techniques. Most of us assume we know what listening is. You heard your boss's order, right? Well, hearing is only the first part of listening. When you physically pick up sound waves with your ears, you are hearing. But listening also involves interpreting what you hear. Then you must evaluate what you have heard, weigh the information, and decide how you'll use it. Finally, on the basis of what you have heard and how you have evaluated the information, you react. So a good listener—and an able negotiator—hears, interprets, evaluates, and reacts.

Because of our misconceptions about what listening really is, we end up doing a pretty poor job of it. Studies show that we spend up to 80 percent of our waking hours communicating, and at least 45 percent of that time is spent listening. Other studies have shown some disturbing facts: Immediately after a 10-minute oral presentation, the average listener understands and properly retains only about half of what was said; within 48 hours, most people retain only 25 percent of the information they heard.

One reason so many people are bad listeners is that they lack training. Consider the four major communication skills we use every day: listening, speaking, reading, and writing. Remember, 45 percent of our time spent communicating involves listening, yet listening is the least-taught communication skill (see Figure 4–1).

Why should we want to become better listeners? Because as the *Challenger* disaster indicates, a failure to listen can cost lives. Listening mistakes can also cost money. If every one of the 100 million–plus workers in the United States were to make a simple

FIGURE 4-1 COMMUNICATIONS SKILLS USED
VERSUS HOW THEY ARE TAUGHT

Communication Skill	Proportion of All Communication Skills Used	Teaching Emphasis Ranking
Reading	19%	1
Writing	22%	2
Speaking	26%	3
Listening	33%	4

$10 listening mistake today, it would cost the country more than $1 billion! Let's make a conservative estimate that most of those 100 million American workers make an average of two listening mistakes a week at a cost of more than $2 billion. If this is true, taken over a year, simple listening mistakes cost us more than $100 billion!

Better listening can mean less paperwork. Most of us learn not to rely on giving information orally because of all the mistakes that result. The result is that we "memo" everything. Just look at your desk. Couldn't some of that paperwork be eliminated by simply talking to another person? Yes, it could, if you could be sure that the other person knew how to listen. All of this unnecessary paperwork means that we need more word processors, use more secretaries' time, and require more file cabinets to store all the notes we write down and get from others. We're not going to magically eliminate the paperwork problem in organizations overnight. But we can improve the situation if we all work to become better listeners.

Leaders should be interested in better listening because it will improve the flow of upward communication. There are a lot of ways we can send messages to the people who work for us but not as many ways for them to communicate upward. Supervisors who don't know how to listen may find that few of their staff members will talk freely to them. This hurts morale and keeps supervisors from receiving all the critical information they need to make effective decisions. Even if the upward flow of communication starts, one bad listener along the way can stop or distort the message.

For negotiators, better listening improves decision making and problem solving. Good listening helps people understand other viewpoints. It also helps keep participants centered on the issue at hand and keeps them from wandering off on irrelevant problems or concerns.

Before suggesting ways we can become better listeners, let's take a short test. Here are the rules. Read the following story once, and only once—don't cheat! This test works best when a friend reads the story to you, after which you take the test.

> You're the manager of a shipping department. One morning the mail brings orders for 25 items. The phone rings and a store orders 10 more items. The buyer from a department store phones and says his store is overstocked, so please cancel his order for 20 items. The boss drops by and says 15 more items should be shipped to another customer. A salesperson comes in and orders 20 items.

Without looking back at the story, answer the following question: What is the name of the shipping manager?

How did you do? If you answered correctly, it's because you followed Rule 1 in developing good listening habits: You resisted distractions. The distractions in this story were all the statistics! Other listening situations may call for you to look past a speaker's bad habits and concentrate on her ideas.

By the way, the correct answer to the test is . . . *your name*. You are the shipping manager!

LISTENING RULES

There are no scientifically documented rules for more effective listening, but if you adopt these commonsense habits, you'll improve your listening ability.

- Ignore distractions.
- Make it personal by asking, "What's in it for me?"
- Focus on content, not delivery.
- Resist the urge to argue or judge until you've heard everything.
- Be alert to central themes, not random facts.

- Take notes if you must, but keep them to a minimum.
- Approach listening as a conscious activity—something you work at.
- Don't react to emotionally charged words or expressions— these will confound your concentration.
- If you want members of your staff to become better listeners, ask for it. Let people know how important listening is. Ask for training to help you and your team develop good listening skills.
- After a negotiating session, hold a listening critique. Ask each person to describe what he or she heard and remembered of the session.

Implement these listening habits and you'll hear more and retain more.

REFLECTIVE LISTENING

There is one listening method that is easy to learn and apply, and that will make you a better listener and a better negotiator. It is called *reflective listening.* This form of listening is different from the way most of us are used to listening, so it may take some practice before you get good at it.

Reflective listening says to the person you're listening to, "I understand what you're saying and how you must feel." It also allows you to check what you believe you heard against what was actually said. This can both build rapport and avoid misunderstandings.

For instance, a coworker angrily tells you that she is having a serious problem with the boss. You reply, "This problem really upsets you, doesn't it?" Your comment assures your friend that you're listening and you care.

Here's an exercise you can do with a team member that will teach both of you how to listen reflectively. Take about five minutes to tell your friend about a problem at work. Your friend should, on occasion, paraphrase back to you what he or she has heard. For example, your friend might say, "So, your boss is not giving you any feedback on how well or poorly you're doing. Do I have that right?" Paraphrasing is nothing more than occasionally repeating in your own words what the other person has said. The listener should demonstrate interest in what you say through a nod, a smile, or a comment such as "I see" or "Tell me more." Your team member, the listener, should avoid trying to solve your problem for you. As a listener, he or she must allow you to discover the answer on your own, which will make you much more committed to the solution! Directly solving another person's problem is *not* reflective listening!

When you and your team member have finished this exercise, discuss how the technique made you, the speaker, feel. Then ask your friend, the reflective listener, how difficult or easy he or she found it to paraphrase. You and your friend will discover that being a good reflective listener requires taking an active part in what some consider a passive activity—listening!

Now reverse roles so that you become the reflective listener and your friend becomes the speaker. Then repeat the discussion following the exercise.

Remember, this is a new way of approaching communication. Expect reflective listening to be difficult the first or second time you do it. But keep in mind the benefits that come from the process.

. . . .

A TIP ON TAKING NOTES

Good listeners give the speaker their full attention. They listen first and evaluate later, and they don't interrupt except to ask for clarification or, as recommended above, to demonstrate interest through paraphrasing. And they keep note taking to a minimum.

. . . .

However, in negotiations it is often useful to write down points of agreement as they are made. "So we agree that after we purchase your company you'll stay on as a part-time consultant at $5,000 per month for six months, is that right?" During the course of a long negotiation, it's easy for one party or the other to forget these minor points, so record them as they are made, and then roll them into the final agreement.

THREE LISTENING QUIZZES

To find out how good a listener you are, take the following three quizzes.

QUIZ ONE

A. Circle the term that best describes you as a listener:

Superior   Excellent   Above Average   Average
Below Average   Poor   Terrible

(Most people would say average or less; only a tiny minority would say superior or excellent)

B. On a scale of 0 to 100 (100 = highest), how would you rate yourself as a listener?

_____

(55 is the self-diagnosed average)

QUIZ TWO

On a scale of 0 to 100, how would the following people rate you as a listener?

Your best friend?
Your boss?
A business colleague?   (The average is around 55)
Your subordinates?   (Again, around 55)
Your spouse?   (Newlyweds rate this category highest; old married couples rate this lowest!)

QUIZ THREE

As a listener, how often do you find yourself engaging in these bad listening habits? Check the appropriate columns. Then tabulate your score using the key below.

Listening Habits	Almost Always	Usually	Some-times	Seldom	Almost Always	Score
1. Calling the subject uninteresting						
2. Criticizing the speaker's delivery or mannerisms						
3. Getting over-stimulated by something speaker says						
4. Listening primarily for facts						
5. Trying to outline everything						
6. Faking attention to the speaker						
7. Allowing interfering distractions						
8. Avoiding difficult material						
9. Letting emotion-charged words arouse antagonism						
10. Daydreaming						

Scoring Key:
Almost Always = 2   Usually = 4   Sometimes = 6   Seldom = 8

The average score is 62. It seems that when we break listening down into specific areas, we rate ourselves higher than when we look at listening in general.

How can you use these quizzes to improve your listening? You need to work on any area where you scored 8 or lower. What are the top four areas you need to work on the most? Seek out help from a coworker who will give you honest feedback.

1. _____

2. _____

3. _____

4. _____

THE COST OF NOT LISTENING

Finally, here's a story that demonstrates the importance of good listening—and the cost of a listening breakdown:

> A down-and-out drifter, hungry for something to eat and willing to work for his meal, walked up to a fancy house. He rang the doorbell and asked the lady of the house for a meal in return for any household chore he could do. "Well, certainly! There is a job you could do for me," the lady said. "Take those two cans of green paint around back and paint my porch." "Be glad to, ma'am," said the drifter. Two hours later, the man returned to the front of the house and said, "Ma'am, I've finished the job, and I'm ready to eat! Oh, by the way, that car I painted was no Porsche; it was a Ferrari!"

By now you should know the importance of and the payoff for having good listening skills. To improve your listening, you have to have a positive attitude and a willingness to work at it. Good listening is not just a matter of hearing.

CHAPTER REVIEW

To discover what you have learned so far, take the following open-book review quiz.

1. What is listening?

_____

2. Name three benefits of better listening for negotiators.

_____

_____

_____

3. Name 5 of the 10 rules of listening, as described in this chapter.

_____

_____

_____

_____

_____

4. What is reflective listening? What are its benefits?

_____

_____

_____

CHAPTER 5

MANAGING CONFLICT

Any time you bring two or more people together to solve a problem or make a decision—or to negotiate—there's a chance of conflict. Indeed, conflict may be the motive for their interaction! Even well-meaning people who seek agreement in good faith can slip into conflict. Why? There are several good reasons. One is the interdependence that exists between people, departments, and organizations; each has unique interests, goals, and plans. Conflicts also arise because negotiators bring different objectives to the table. Achieving one objective may result in non-achievement of the other—an objective that someone values. Other reasons for conflict include competition for resources, personal antagonisms, and organizational turf warfare.

Unmanaged conflict is often costly. It can divert energy, time, and resources from legitimate and important personal and organizational goals and motivate sabotage by disaffected parties. At a personal level, intense conflict can produce stress, which, in turn, may lead to health and emotional problems.

Conflict, if handled right, can be a good thing.

A skillfully handled conflict, on the other hand, can be beneficial. It can function as a safety valve, allowing people to vent their frustrations; and it can lead to solutions for troublesome problems.

Conflict avoidance seldom results in problem resolution or needed change. Few conflicts go away of their own accord. But effective conflict management can lead to increased cohesion and loyalty. Facing problems together often brings people closer, as when two parties spend time and energy trying to negotiate a deal. Consider the example of more than a decade of negotiations that took place between leaders of Northern Ireland's Protestant majority, and the Catholic minority's Sinn Fein. These parties had been mortal enemies for as long as anyone cared to remember. Conflict and outright hatred had been practically baked into the genetic code of Northern Ireland's divided populous. But those years of negotiation had forced leaders of the two sides to know one another, to appreciate their aspirations, and to develop trust. That trust led to a political power-sharing agreement that transferred control of the region's governmental departments to a 12-member administration representing the once-polarized parties.

QUIZ: HOW DO YOU NATURALLY HANDLE CONFLICT?

To learn how to manage conflict effectively, it's a good idea to understand how you personally handle conflict. Are you a conflict avoider? Are you uncompromising in dealing with conflict? Do you roll over in the face of conflict? Taking the following quiz will help you answer these questions.

Directions: Read the statements in Figure 5–1 and then circle only the numbers next to the questions that describe how you handle conflict. For instance, if you agree with the first statement in the survey, circle both numbers to the right of the question (1 and 1). When you're finished, add up all' the circled numbers under "concern for people" and divide that number by the number of

FIGURE 5-1

	Concern for People	Concern for Production
1. Maintains neutrality at all costs; views conflict as a worthless and punishing experience (w/a)	1	1
2. Feels a high concern for people regardless of the production of results and therefore tries to smooth over or ignore conflicts in an attempt to keep everybody happy (s/a)	9	1
3. Views production of results (usually his or her own personal goals) as much more important than people and sees nothing wrong with using force when necessary (f/c)	1	9
4. Believes that everyone should have an equal chance to express opinions (c)	5	5
5. Gives equal consideration to people and production of results (ps/c)	9	9
6. Removes self either physically or mentally from groups experiencing any type of conflict; stays away from any situation that might possibly produce conflict (w/a)	1	1
7. Believes that surface harmony is important to maintain good relationships and receive personal acceptance; has motto of "If you can't say something nice, don't say anything at all" (s/a)	9	1
8. Views conflict as a win-lose situation or as a power struggle in which one person must fail so that the other can succeed; not possible to compromise (f/c)	1	9
9. Tries to find a solution that everyone can live with (c)	5	5
10. Views conflict as beneficial if handled in an open manner; lays all cards on the table (ps/c)	9	9
11. Feels little concern for people or production of results but has great desire for noninvolvement (w/a)	1	1
12. Views open conflict as destructive; gives in to the will of others if necessary (s/a)	9	1
13. Has great respect for power and submits to arbitration only because the arbitrator's power is greater (f/c)	1	9
14. Uses voting or other methods of compromise as a way to avoid direct confrontation; believes that a high-quality solution is not as important as a workable or agreeable solution (c)	5	5
15. Attempts to reach a consensus agreement; is willing to spend a great deal of time and effort to achieve it (ps/c)	9	9
A. Total each column score	_____	_____
B. Averages	_____	_____

(column total divided by number of questions answered)

questions you agreed with. Then add up all the circled numbers under "concern for production" and divide by the number of questions you agreed with. You will then have an average score for "concern for people" and an average score for "concern for production." Then plot your average conflict scores on the table at the end of the survey.

Now, plot your averages on the table in Figure 5–2. If your average people-production scores were close to 1, 1, you prefer a "withdrawal/avoidance" (w/a) or win-lose conflict style.

If your average people-production scores were close to 9, 1, you prefer a "forcing" (f) or win-lose conflict style.

If your average people-production scores were close to 9, 9, you prefer a "problem-solving/collaboration" (ps/c) or win-win conflict style.

If your average people-production scores were close to 5, you prefer a "compromising" (c) or lose-lose conflict style.

Are you locked in to a particular style? No. As with the communication styles quiz you took earlier, your goal should be to find out what style you naturally prefer and learn how to "flex" to another style as required by circumstances.

FIGURE 5-2 CONFLICT RESOLUTION STYLES

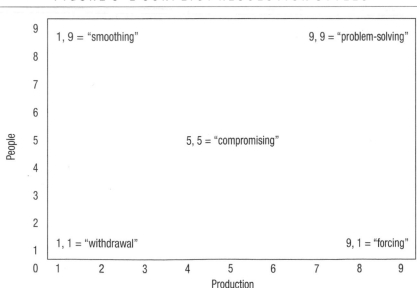

WHEN TO USE EACH OF THE FIVE STYLES OF CONFLICT RESOLUTION

Following are some example scenarios of when it would be appropriate to use each of the five styles shown in Figure 5–2.

Strategy #1: Withdrawal/Avoidance

Withdrawal/avoidance is a strategy that calls for ignoring conflict in the hope that it will go away. People who practice this style maintain neutrality at all costs and view conflict as a worthless and punishing exercise. They remove themselves physically or mentally from the situation and feel little concern for people and for task accomplishment. People who follow the withdrawal/avoidance strategy want to steer clear of conflict.

Although you might think this is not an effective strategy, it is the best strategy to use:

- When the issues are trivial
- When the conflicted parties lack conflict management skills
- When the potential losses in the conflict outweigh the potential gains (based on a simple "cost-benefit" analysis)
- When there is not enough time to work through the issues at the heart of the conflict

The drawback of using withdrawal/avoidance, of course, is that it only delays the confrontation!

Strategy #2: Smoothing/Accommodation

Adherents of this strategy feel a greater concern for people than for getting what they or their organization needs. They try to smooth over or ignore conflict to keep everybody happy. They see conflict as destructive and will give in to others if necessary to maintain the peace.

Smoothing or accommodation may be the best strategy to use:

■ When the issues are minor

■ When damage to the relationship will hurt all parties involved in a conflict

■ When there is a need to temporarily reduce the level of conflict in order to get more information or to get certain tasks done

■ When tempers are so hot that no progress can be made

What is the drawback of using smoothing or accommodation? It offers only a temporary solution—sort of like putting a Band-Aid on a major wound. More important, the interests of the accommodator—the "appeaser"—will get shortchanged.

Strategy #3: Compromising

Compromisers try to find solutions that everybody can live with. They will advocate voting as a way of avoiding direct conflict and believe that a high-quality solution is not as important as a solution everybody can live with.

When should you compromise?

■ When an ideal solution isn't needed

■ When you need a temporary solution for a complex problem

■ When both sides have equal power

The problem with compromise is that everybody loses something (that is the definition of compromise). You probably won't reach the best solution through compromise. Remember the expression, "A half loaf is better than no loaf at all." Compromise will get you that half loaf when the outcome you seek is a whole loaf.

Strategy #4: Forcing/Competition

People who prefer a forcing or competition strategy see reaching their own goals as all important—to heck with the other side. They see conflict as a win-lose situation in which their opponents must lose for them to win. They submit to arbitration only when they lack the power to do otherwise.

When should you use a forcing or competitive style?

■ When you or the group needs an immediate action or decision

■ When all parties in a conflict expect and appreciate the use of power and force

■ When all parties in a conflict understand and accept the power relationship between them

■ When there is no expectation of a long-term relationship with the other side

There are drawbacks to using forcing or competition. The real cause of the conflict remains unresolved, and whatever solution is achieved will only be temporary. You also have to consider the emotions of the loser, who will probably seek revenge when he or she sees the opportunity. The loser may be in a weak power position today, but who knows about tomorrow?

Strategy #5: Problem Solving/Collaboration

People who follow a problem-solving or collaborative strategy give equal consideration to people and to results and view conflict as beneficial if handled in an open manner. Open and honest communication ("laying all the cards on the table") is a key characteristic and necessary component of this strategy. Its practitioners aim for consensus in solving the problem and are willing to spend a lot of time to achieve that consensus.

When should you use problem solving or collaboration? These styles are effective:

■ When everybody in the conflict is trained in problem-solving methods

■ When the parties have common goals

■ When the conflict results from a simple misunderstanding or lack of communication

■ When the parties expect to have a long-term relationship

The problem-solving or collaboration strategy is usually the best approach to win-win negotiations, but it has drawbacks. It will not work with people who have different values or goals. It will not work, for instance, if your negotiating partner has adopted the old Soviet approach—namely, "What's ours is ours; what's yours is negotiable." You need a different strategy when dealing with people like that.

Another drawback is that problem solving is time-consuming. The Protestants and Catholics of Northern Ireland, for example, spent almost 10 years resolving their issues. If the group or situation calls for a fast decision, you may have to use a forcing style.

HOW DO YOU USE A PROBLEM-SOLVING (WIN-WIN) STRATEGY?

The problem-solving (collaboration) strategy is usually the best way to cut through conflict, make decisions, and work toward win-win deals. But what's the best way to go about it? The answer is the *reflective thinking process*.

The reflective thinking process can be a powerful "win-win" tool.

The reflective thinking process is a powerful win-win negotiating tool that can empower everybody involved in a negotiation to learn to agree honestly about things that affect them. It generally produces results that are better than alternative strategies, more effective decisions, and a high degree of buy-in among participants.

The reflective thinking process has five important steps:

1. **Identify the problem**. If you're part of a group, identifying the problem may take some open and honest discussion. Is what

you've identified really the problem or merely a symptom of a problem? Does this problem identification satisfy your needs? Is your problem identification clear and concise to the point where you could explain it easily to an intelligent stranger?

2. **Brainstorm a list of possible solutions**. This is an easy and practical technique that anybody can use. Take out a sheet of paper (or use a flipchart, overhead, or blackboard that all can see). Write down all the possible solutions you or the group can think of. Do not allow any negative comments about these ideas. You are going after a quantity of ideas, regardless of quality. The more ideas, the better. Once you've run out of new ideas, you or the group should combine ideas that are essentially the same. Then start to weed out clearly unworkable ideas until you get four or five alternative solutions that you or the group could live with.

3. **Evaluate alternative solutions**. A technique called force field analysis (see Figure 5–3) can help you with this step. Take out another sheet of paper, draw a line down the middle, and label one column with a plus sign (+) and the other with a minus sign (–), symbolizing benefits and risks. Then generate all the positives and negatives associated with each solution developed in step two.

4. **Make a decision**. There are three ways you can decide which alternative to use. Voting is one method. It's fast, but what

FIGURE 5-3 FORCE FIELD ANALYSIS

Alternatives	(+) Positives	(–) Negatives
Solution 1		
Solution 2		
Solution 3		
Solution 4		
Solution 5		

about the people in a group who end up on the losing end of the vote? They may become powerful resisters to whatever decision is made in this way.

A second possibility is consensus, the preferred method for group decision making most of the time. Consensus, or talking out the alternatives until everybody decides on a best solution, produces a decision with a high degree of member support. However, consensus does take time, as many readers who have served on juries may know. If time is important, consensus may not be possible.

The third method is a hybrid decision-making method sometimes called the nominal group technique (NGT), in which all members involved in a problem individually rank order their preferences. The rankings are then averaged. The group agrees ahead of time that the alternative that receives the highest average ranking will be the group decision. Use NGT when your group becomes deadlocked. It's not as good as consensus but it's better than voting because it yields a higher degree of commitment from group members than voting. A drawback of NGT is that it is time-consuming, although less so than consensus.

5. **Monitor the results of the chosen solution**. This is a crucial step in group decision making. The tendency for some groups, especially groups that have fought in the past, is to skip this step. They are so often relieved that they made a decision without fighting and yelling that they forget to do it! Monitoring begins with planning. How will the group monitor the result? Should it check every month, every quarter, every year? Who will do what when, where, and how? Make sure the group agrees ahead of time how to monitor the solution chosen. This bit of preplanning will save time and disagreement down the road.

The reflective thinking method is very effective in most cases. Framing the conflict as "us versus the problem" instead of "us versus them" leads to a win-win outcome. However, there are some situations where the reflective thinking method may not be the best way to make decisions or solve problems.

Imagine, for example, a navy ship whose captain is a big believer in participative management and who regularly uses the reflective thinking model in solving problems aboard ship. The officers under the captain's command enjoy having a say in decisions that affect them and their sailors. And it's a good way for the captain to develop the leadership skills of his officers. Then one day, the ship strays into enemy waters and is torpedoed and quickly lists badly to port. Should the captain call the ship's officers together and follow the reflective thinking model in deciding what to do? Or does the situation require another approach? The captain could follow the reflective thinking model of decision making. Everybody on board would feel good about the process. But they would also probably drown. Perhaps both the officers and sailors would appreciate the captain's use of an authoritative decision-making method: "You radio for help! You take charge of fire control! You lower the lifeboats!"

Reflective thinking is a practical method for producing high-quality decisions that everybody can support, but as the ship example illustrates, it's not best in every situation. If used improperly, the reflective thinking process can make you appear indecisive. More than three quarters of the decisions most of us have to make can and should be made on the spot, while perhaps 15 percent need some time and thought, and 5 percent of the decisions shouldn't have to be made at all.

CHAPTER REVIEW

To discover what you have learned in this chapter, take the following open-book review quiz.

1. Can conflict ever be good? Why or why not?

_____

_____

2. How do you naturally handle conflict? Which one of the five styles is closest to your style?

_____

_____

3. Why should you first try for a win-win agreement?

_____

_____

CHAPTER 6

THE IMPORTANCE OF ASSERTIVENESS

C onflict is present or potentially present in most negotiations. The previous chapter explained generic strategies you can adopt to deal with conflict. This one moves down to the personal level, to what you can do to be more successful in conflicted situations, especially when you must deal with difficult people. The first step is to learn to be more assertive.

People characteristically deal with others by assuming one of the four roles described in Figure 6–1: the Passive Wimp, the Manipulative Weasel, the Win-Win Team Player, and the Bully. These ways of dealing with others fall between the extremes of passivity and aggression. People who adopt the first approach, the Passive Wimp, are likely to end up as roadkill in the course of strenuous negotiations, especially when they go head-to-head with a Bully. To achieve their goals they must rely on the generosity of others.

To be successful, a negotiator must muster an appropriate level of assertiveness.

FIGURE 6-1 FOUR WAYS OF DEALING WITH OTHERS

Passive ———————————————————————————— Aggressive

Nonassertive	Indirect	Assertive	Aggressive
Passive Wimp	Manipulative Weasel	Win-Win Team Player	Bully
Self-denying, placating, submissive, avoiding; soft voice; downcast eyes; doormat	Sneaky, coy, seductive, vindictive, revengeful; chooses for others	Stands up for own rights while respecting others'; makes own choices	Denies others' rights; dominating; demanding; judgmental; chooses for others

Quiz: How Assertive Are You?

Respond to each item with a yes or no. Then check your score with the key at the end of the quiz. This quiz will let you know if you need to work on being more assertive.

1. I state my own view when someone with more authority disagrees with me.
2. I express irritation if someone with whom I am speaking begins talking to someone else in the middle of our conversation.
3. I insist that the landlord or repairperson make timely repairs.
4. I openly express love and affection and tell people that I care for them.
5. I make direct eye contact when speaking with others.
6. When a person is being highly unfair, I call it to his or her attention.
7. I ask friends for small favors or help.
8. I say no without apology if people make unreasonable demands of me.
9. At work, I suggest new procedures or ways of doing things.
10. I cut short telephone calls when I am busy.
11. I am able to refuse unreasonable requests made by others.
12. I look for a seat in the front of a crowded room rather than stand in the back.
13. If someone keeps kicking the back of my chair, I ask him or her to stop.
14. I can speak in front of a group without becoming overly anxious.
15. I have confidence in my own judgment.
16. I seek repayment from a friend who borrowed $20 and has forgotten to repay me.
17. I stay calm when others are scrutinizing my work or reviewing it.
18. I speak up in a meeting if I feel that my idea is relevant.
19. I do not apologize for what I am about to say.

(continued)

20. I ask a friend who keeps calling me very late at night not to call after a certain time.
21. When merchandise is faulty, I return it for adjustment.
22. I can ask for a raise or promotion without feeling overly anxious.
23. I speak firmly and loudly enough to be heard and understood.
24. I state my own and others' limitations without feeling guilty.
25. When I meet someone for the first time, I introduce myself and extend my hand.
26. I can work with others without trying to make them feel guilty or manipulated.
27. I express my opinions rather than keep them to myself.
28. In a restaurant, if my meal is unacceptable, I ask the waiter to correct it.
29. I am able to confront an issue or problem at work rather than call in sick.
30. I insist that my spouse or roommate take on a fair share of the household chores.

Total YES _____   Total NO _____

Scoring Key:
22 or more yes responses = You're assertive enough
15–21 yes responses = You have some areas to work on
Fewer than 15 yes responses = You're the mayor of Wimp City!

Once you know you're assertive enough—that you stand up for your rights, are diplomatic, and have a win-win problem-solving orientation—you can use a variety of tactics to handle difficult people and situations. But first, when should you draw on your assertive powers? There are some typical situations where assertiveness pays off—and each will involve negotiations on your part:

■ A person's performance is hindering achievement of group goals. For example, Joanne's disruptive behavior is negatively affecting your group's work. You must assertively intervene.

■ A person's actions are adversely impacting your own success. This is a case of the same thing but hits closer to home. When a person does something that causes you harm, you have to tell yourself, "I cannot afford to ignore this."

■ A problem with an employee or a customer keeps reappearing despite your offhanded attempts to fix it. In the past you were reluctant to tackle the problem directly, fearful that doing so would open a Pandora's box of other troubles. But remember, by doing nothing, you'll probably only make matters worse.

Before confronting another person, make sure you aren't contributing to the problem. What part of the situation might you be contributing to? What can you do about it?

> **Before confronting another person, make sure you aren't contributing to the problem.**

SIX WAYS TO ASSERTIVELY HANDLE CONFLICT

Left alone, serious conflict will fester. Someone has to step up to it and move it toward resolution. Consider the following six approaches.

#1: Confront Gently

This technique calls for openly confronting the situation, but in a diplomatic manner. You'll know that you are being successful at gentle confrontation if you can answer yes to all three of these questions: Has the other person's behavior changed? Have you preserved the self-esteem of the other person? Have you preserved the relationship?

Here's how to prepare for gentle confrontation:

- Maintain control of your emotions. Avoid overreacting.
- Rehearse what you plan to say. Practice makes perfect.
- Make sure you're aware and in control of your voice, body, and facial expression.
- Be willing to listen—and don't interrupt while the other person is telling his side of the story.

There are six elements to constructive *assertive but gentle* confrontation. These are widely taught to new supervisors and managers but can be applied to negotiating situations in which the behavior of the other side is getting in the way of a good outcome:

1. Objectively describe the undesirable behavior you're trying to change. Do not be subjective; do not be personal.

2. Identify the specific and negative tangible effects of the behavior. Don't attack the person—that will only put him or her on the defensive. Instead, attack the problem. For example, don't say, "Your frequent tardiness tells me that you don't think our meetings are important." Instead say, "Your coming late makes it impossible for the other people on this panel to get their work done."

3. Don't lecture. Nothing turns people off more than being talked down to, lecture style.

4. Listen to the other person's response; don't be tempted to interrupt.

5. Describe your future expectations in specific terms.

6. Gain commitment or agreement from the other person. Either you can ask him if he agrees, or you can say, "This seems like a reasonable request, doesn't it?" While you're saying this, look the other person in the eye, and look for agreement.

Most people want to be reasonable. Getting the other side to agree that you are being reasonable can be a powerful tool in resolving conflict—with either a problem employee or a difficult negotiating counterpart. It can move the other side to show reasonableness as well, and that may mean a bigger concession to you in the future.

Most people want to be reasonable.

With that advice in mind, how would you tackle the following situation:

> Your team is negotiating to buy a large allotment of jet fuel. Jerry, one of the sellers, has raised and lowered the price of the fuel several times without explanation. How can you handle this situation using the assertive confrontation model?

Hint: Be polite. Be specific. Describe the effects of those erratic price changes on your business—and your ability to remain a customer. Then ask for something specific. Ask for commitment.

#2: Say No Assertively

One test of assertiveness is the ability to say no. Do you often find yourself saying yes to requests when you really want to say no? Are people always asking you for many small concessions because you're a pushover? If so, you need to be assertive—to stand up for your interests and say no. Using the principles of assertive confrontation, how would you say no in the following cases?

■ **The demanding customer.** You must refuse the other side's demand for an extended warranty on the framing implements you're trying to sell because such a practice is not followed in your industry.

Hint: First, explain that your boss would never agree to such a demand. Second, offer an alternative (people are more likely to agree with you if you offer them an alternative). Perhaps you could extend such an unprecedented warranty if the other side locks in to a longer-term contract. Third, ask for commitment and understanding. The wrong way to respond is to say, "I said no. What part of no don't you understand?" Put yourself on the receiving end of that message. How would it make you feel? Keep in mind that you want to say no but at the same time preserve the relationship.

■ **The boss asks for too much.** Your boss has just asked you to stay late again to work on a proposal that is due. You don't mind pitching in when there are emergencies, but her requests for working after hours have become routine. If you don't push back, you're afraid you'll soon have a 10-hour-per-day job.

Hint: State, "I understand that the proposal is important. As you know, I've stayed late three nights in a row to work on this.

But tonight I have important family business I must attend to. However, I'd be glad to come in a half hour early tomorrow to work on the project. Doesn't that seem fair to you?"

#3: Disarm the Opposition

Sometimes the other person has a legitimate beef. If you deny that reality, the other person will be angry and the problem will get worse. By acknowledging that the other person is right, you will have taken an important step toward diffusing the crisis. Let's assume that a police officer pulls you over for speeding (yes, you were driving too fast).

Usual Defensive Approach

You: What's the problem? I wasn't speeding. My friend sitting right
   here will vouch for me.
Police officer: Don't tell me that. My speedometer doesn't lie.

How would you disarm the opposition?

_____

_____

What might the officer say?

_____

_____

   Hint: Surprise the officer. He expects you to deny that you were speeding. Admit it. You can use the same technique while negotiating. Just don't overdo it; if you get predictable, you'll lose effectiveness.

#4: Handle Your Anger

Tough negotiations often generate friction, which easily takes the form of anger. Anger in turn makes what might have been a win-

win negotiation a win-lose contest, which isn't good for either side—particularly for the one with the weakest negotiating hand. So do whatever you can to diffuse anger. Never tell another person, "Don't be angry." Instead, encourage the person to tell you what's angering her.

There are some things to do with an angry person:

- Listen. Maybe the person has a right to be angry.

- Don't argue, even if that is what the person wants. A person's feelings are neither right nor wrong. Perhaps the other person's self-esteem is in the Dumpster. Compliment him whenever possible.

- Ask open-ended questions—not yes/no questions—to uncover the reason for the person's anger.

- Demonstrate empathy. Use the reflective listening technique of occasionally paraphrasing the other person's words.

- If you're in the wrong, admit it!

- Encourage cheerfulness, and use light humor whenever possible.

But the other side isn't always the angry party. You may be the angry one. If you feel you're in danger of really exploding in anger, consider these suggestions:

- Go for a walk by yourself to get away from the problem for a while. That separation may clear the way for more constructive, positive thinking.

- Write an angry letter—but don't send it. Writing the letter will get the anger out of your system without hurting anybody. It will also force you to clarify your complaint.

- Then write a calmer, more rational letter. Either send it to the person who angers you or use the act of writing as a rehearsal for facing the individual in person.

What should you do if the rational approach doesn't work and the other side is dismissive of whatever is upsetting you? Sometimes a good old-fashioned temper tantrum on your part will focus people's attention on a problem. This works best if you have a reputation for being a rational, cool customer. Do it only to get people's attention on a problem; be selective about using this drastic measure (if you overuse it, you'll just be seen as a hothead). Even then don't make it personal. Direct your anger at the situation, not at the other person.

. . . .

Consider the following situation. You must straighten out a problem with somebody from the other negotiating team, and you're sure that dealing with that person will make you angry. And your anger will make matters worse. What should you do?

_____

_____

Hint: Let the person know you're angry. Be specific about describing what you think is wrong. Stick to talking about actions and behaviors, not about attitudes or motivations. Listen. Look for solutions to the problem so that everybody wins. You can influence and persuade others by not yelling and by remaining in control.

#5: Appeal to a Powerful Third Party

Sometimes a gentle approach to a problem won't work. The other person may not want to compromise; he may not be interested in finding a win-win solution to the conflict. He may want to use power to solve the conflict. In that case, you may have to do the same—by appealing to a more powerful third party. Use this tactic only when winning is *very* important, because it will certainly create ill will. Here are two examples of appealing to a third party:

1. Your company is involved in a labor dispute that, after being stonewalled by the local union, you take to the state labor board. This third party will impose a settlement that may please neither side.

2. You have reached an impasse with the person with whom you are negotiating a supplier contract. As a longtime supplier, you've always enjoyed an amiable relationship with this company, and its contracts have always benefited both parties. But the new purchasing manager seems cut from different cloth. He is being extremely unreasonable, pressing you so severely on price that you will be unable to make any money on your sales to his company. You wonder if this newcomer is trying to impress his boss with his negotiating toughness at your expense. So you take a drastic step: You contact his superior and ask, "as a longtime and reliable supplier to your corporation," that you be allowed to bring in someone else to negotiate with you.

#6: Trade Places with Your Antagonist

One of the most effective ways of diffusing conflict is to get each party to walk a mile or two in the other person's shoes. You can do this through a role-playing exercise in which each party adopts the other person's perspective and interests. If done well, this exercise sensitizes each of the parties to the other's concerns and helps each understand the source of conflict.

To use this strategy, ask the other person to (a) write down *her* side of the dispute, and (b) write a paragraph in which she describes *your* viewpoint—as she understands it. Then, you do the same. Now, exchange the written information and discuss the differences. Once you've done that, trade places, with you arguing her point of view and she arguing yours. This is a powerful exercise when both parties take it seriously and do their best to represent the views of the other side.

CHAPTER REVIEW

To find out what you have learned so far, take the following open-book review quiz.

1. When can conflict be good?

_____

2. How do you handle conflict?

_____

_____

3. What are the three kinds of conflict resolution? What is the win-win outcome? Why is it normally the preferable outcome?

_____

_____

4. Why is assertiveness preferable to any other way of dealing with others?

_____

5. How would you gently confront a problem person?

_____

_____

6. How should you deal with anger?

_____

_____

7. What should you do about temper tantrums?

_____

CHAPTER 7

PREPARE TO NEGOTIATE

N ow that you've acquainted yourself with the background skills of negotiating, it's time to get down to business. This chapter and those that follow cover the basic "to do" items that every negotiator must undertake, beginning with preparation.

Like every other important task, preparation provides a foundation for success. You want to go into your negotiation as well prepared as you can be. Don't even think about "winging" it. If you're lucky, that's what the other side will do. To be prepared, you must:

■ Identify issues and interests.

■ Develop a mental picture of an ideal agreement.

■ Determine your alternatives to a deal and reserve price and try to do the same for the other side.

■ Improve your negotiating position.

UNDERSTAND ISSUES AND INTERESTS

The starting point of preparation is a thorough understanding of the issues and of the interests of all parties to the deal. Consider the example of a small company that plans to negotiate the purchase of a new office server and PC network. The manager in charge might prepare by drawing up a document like the one shown in Figure 7–1, based on his knowledge of the situation and whatever he can learn about the equipment vendor (e.g., through discussions with the vendor's sales reps and so forth). There he identifies the issues that matter to his company, and those most likely to matter to the equipment vendor.

Issues describe what's important in this particular deal—what's at stake. Interests are similar but are more general. They are related to the long-term well-being of the negotiating parties. If you understand issues and interests very well—and prioritize them in order of importance—you'll be in a much better position to horse-trade with the other side.

FIGURE 7-1 ISSUES AND INTERESTS

	Our Company	The Equipment Vendor
Issues	1. A system that meets IT needs for less than $80K 2. System reliability 3. Payment terms 4. Timing of delivery and installation	1. A profitable sale 2. Creditworthiness of the customer
Interests	1. Costs 2. Reliability (downtime creates chaos) 3. Long-term relationship with a supplier that can provide training, maintenance, and upgrades that will enhance our chances of business success	1. A profitable transaction 2. Long-term relationship with a customer that will pay for maintenance and future upgrades

Common interests indicate a potential win-win deal.

Notice in Figure 7–1 how the two parties have a mutual interest in a long-term business relationship. This is a signal that a win-win negotiation is possible. Each party might be willing to trade off something to serve that interest. For example, the buyer might not select the vendor with the lowest price. He might opt for a vendor that offers a reasonable price if the vendor appears to be the better long-term supplier. For its part, the equipment vendor may give up something on the selling price in anticipation of other opportunities of serving the customer in the years ahead: a maintenance contract, the sale of system upgrades, etc.

. . . .

TIP: LEARN AS MUCH AS POSSIBLE ABOUT THE OTHER SIDE.

As you prepare, learn as much as you can about the organization and the individuals with whom you will be dealing. The more information you have, the better. Know your negotiating partner's background and personal characteristics (emotional and personal needs, involvement in office politics). Also, find out how much this person wants what he or she is fighting for. The more a person wants one thing, the more likely he or she is to make concessions on others.

. . . .

Are you currently embroiled in a negotiation, or do you anticipate being so in the near future? Then take a few minutes to jot down the issues and interests that matter most. Prioritize them.

_____

_____

_____

Now, based on what you know, do the same for the other negotiating party or parties. If you don't know their issues and interests, investigate.

_____

_____

_____

What sources of information do you need to tap on your opponent?

_____

_____

DEVELOP A MENTAL PICTURE OF AN IDEAL AGREEMENT

Once you understand the issues at stake and interests of the negotiating parties, develop a mental picture of an ideal agreement. What would be the best takeaway for you? And if you understand the interests of the other side, how would they see the ideal resolution?

In cases where mutual interest can be found, as shown in Figure 7–1, think about things that you could trade off, at little expense to yourself, for things that the other side might find highly valuable. For instance, if you were the vendor in our example and had lots of techies with time on their hands this month, you might say, "If we can negotiate the purchase before the end of the month, I'd be willing to have two of our people spend three to four days training your personnel. They'll teach them what they need to know to get the most out of your new system—and at no extra cost to you." Here, you saw a chance to sweeten the deal with something of little value to yourself (excess techie time), but that your customer values highly (technical training). In exchange, you'll get something you value: a sale this month.

. . . .

Take a moment to identify something *you* value little (e.g., excess capacity), but your negotiating partner would dearly like to have. Does your negotiating partner have something she values little, but you'd like to have?

DETERMINE YOUR ALTERNATIVES AND RESERVE PRICE

What is your best alternative if your current negotiations fail? What is the price (reserve price) at which you'd be willing to walk away? Chapter 2 discussed these concepts in detail. Never walk into a negotiation without having these in your head. If you are part of a negotiating team, the team must be in agreement on these. Write them down here.

. . . .

Our best alternative is _____

. . . .

Remember: Anyone who enters a negotiation with no feasible alternative is at the mercy of the other side. He or she is doomed to be a deal taker, not a deal maker.

. . . .

Our reserve price is _____

. . . .

Now put yourself in the shoes of the person with whom you plan to negotiate and determine that person's best alternative and reserve price. This may require some investigation, but time spent doing this is worthwhile. Having an informed view of the other side's best alternative and reserve price is analogous to knowing which cards the other side holds in a game of poker. If you find yourself in a win-lose negotiation, you'll know when to push, when to back off, and when to bluff.

IMPROVE YOUR NEGOTIATING POSITION

Imagine that your team is scheduled to run a 10-mile road race against a team from another company—and the race date is two months from today. And the stakes are high. Would you just show up and do the best you can, or would you start training tomorrow?

If you were serious about winning, you'd use every day over the next two months to build the speed and endurance of your team. And if you were clever and mischievous, you would do something to weaken your opponents, such as sending them a large daily batch of sugar donuts with a note reading, "With Our Best Wishes." Those daily donuts would hit them like a ton of bricks somewhere around mile five of the race! Better yet, you could weaken the other team by recruiting its fastest member to your team.

Negotiation preparation is no different. You want to strengthen your position and, if possible, weaken the position of the other side (particularly if you anticipate a win-lose slugfest). How can this be done? Here are a few suggestions:

■ **Strengthen your best alternative to a deal.** You already know your best alternative to a negotiated deal with the other side, but that shouldn't stop you from seeking even better alternatives. Consider this example:

> Sarah wants to buy a brand-new sedan. Her local dealer insists that $19,000 is as low as he can go in selling the model she wants. Her best alternative at this point is to simply do nothing—that is, to keep driving her old clunker. But she worries that her car is too unreliable for the driving she plans to do. Thus, she is in a weak bargaining position. Determined to do better, Sarah does her homework and finds a neighbor who owns a like-new version of the same sedan that he's willing to sell for only $16,000. "My boss just gave me a company car," he says, "so I really don't need this one anymore. It has only 20,500 miles on the odometer."

In this example, a little homework helped Sarah to improve her position. With a stronger alternative, she can go back to the auto dealer and negotiate from a position of greater strength. If he won't budge from $19,000, she knows that she can walk away and buy the neighbor's model for less.

> As you prepare, try to strengthen your position—or weaken your opponent's.

■ **Weaken the other side's position.** This is generally more difficult, but still possible. Consider this example:

Harold is the vice president of new product development for an athletic shoe company. He has developed a plan for a new line of running shoes. But in selling the CEO on the plan he has run into fierce resistance from the chief financial officer. "What's the point," the financial guy tells the CEO. "We'll spend nearly a million dollars on product development and marketing, and if we're successful, we simply will have cannibalized our current sales. Every dollar in sales we win with the new product line will eliminate a dollar of sales from our existing products."

Harold understood that the CFO had more influence with the CEO than he did, so he was unlikely to win his case unless he could somehow undermine the CFO's position and improve his own. Toward that end he enlisted the support of the company's vice president of sales and marketing, who had considerable influence with the CEO. That VP went to bat for the new product line, essentially neutralizing the influence of the CFO, and putting Harold into a much stronger negotiating position.

This example illustrates a practice that weaker parties can use to tip the balance of influence away from their negotiating adversaries: the formation of coalitions. If you find yourself in a weak position, try to find allies. Your combined strength may put you in a dominant position. If you recruit an ally from the opponent's camp, the effect will be magnified.

. . . .

This chapter has described four practical things you can do to prepare for negotiations. The next chapter offers equally practical tactics you can use to reach a favorable agreement. But before you move on, take a moment to review what you've learned.

CHAPTER REVIEW

To discover what you have learned so far, take the following open-book review quiz.

1. As you prepare, why is It useful to identify the interests of the other side?

_____

_____

_____

2. Think for a moment about your most recently concluded negotiation. Was there anything under your control that had little value for you but that the other side would have valued greatly? Could you have traded off that thing for something the other side controlled? Explain.

_____

_____

_____

3. Think about whatever matter you are currently negotiating—with your boss, a family member, a customer, or someone else. What is the best alternative available to you if that negotiation fails?

_____

_____

_____

4. Following up on Question #3, what could you have done to strengthen your best
   alternative?

   _____

   _____

   _____

CHAPTER 8

DOING THE DEAL

N ow that you've acquainted yourself with the skills and prepa-
ratory activities that support effective negotiating, let's move
toward actual practice. This chapter covers two important
topics: the series of ordered steps that negotiations typically go
through from beginning to end, and a handful of practical tactics
you can apply as you go through them.

THE FIVE BASIC STEPS

Negotiating is like a ritual that generally proceeds through an ordered set of steps:

1.   Getting to know each other

2.   Beginning negotiations

3.   Expressing disagreement and conflict

4.   Reassessing and compromising

5.   Reaching agreement

In reality, negotiations rarely follow a neat, linear progression. For instance, "getting to know each other" is not confined to the beginning of the process; the savvy negotiator continues to learn more about the other side until the very end. Likewise, disagreement and conflict are liable to occur at any time. Nevertheless, learning the five steps is a useful way for novices to familiarize themselves with the entire process.

Step 1: Getting to Know Each Other

Although there's a temptation to jump right into negotiations, it is important for negotiators to spend some time getting to know each other. This is particularly true when you are dealing with people from Asian and Latin American cultural backgrounds, where trust based on relationships is essential. It is during this period that you'll have a chance to learn more about what is important to the other side—their *issues and interests*. Check what you learn against the issues and interests you assumed during the preparation stage. This is also a time to assess the personalities of the individuals involved. Getting to know one another at a personal level is the first step toward building trust, an important factor in successful negotiating.

Trust is an important factor in successful negotiating.

One of the things you'll want to learn about the people on the other side is their *authority to make a deal.* Are you dealing with people who can make the ultimate decisions and commitments for their side, or are you dealing with low-level functionaries who'll eventually say, "I can't agree to that unless I first check with my boss." Some parties will negotiate as a ploy to determine your position and then tell you they don't have the authority to accept your terms. They'll then go to another person (their boss or some other "higher-up") who will reject what you've negotiated and try to get a better deal. Obviously you want to deal with people who have the authority to decide and to commit. In fact, you should insist on it.

For example, if you are the CEO of your organization, you don't want to negotiate with middle managers from the other side. You should insist on dealing with someone with equal stature and decision-making authority.

Step 2: Beginning Negotiations

Some negotiations are easy; some are very complex. You may not know which you're up against until negotiations are under way and you and the other side have shared goals. "We would like to come away from these discussions with an agreement that will provide our factory with the components it needs, when it needs them, and at a price we can afford. What is your goal?" The other side may have hidden goals that only come out later in the process.

Goals may be bundled together ("Let's discuss both X and Y") or separated ("Let's have separate negotiations for X and Y"). If you've done your homework, you will have already decided where the advantage lies for you on bundling or separating issues.

Experts disagree on whether to try to begin negotiations with a minor issue or a major one. Some say that settling a minor issue creates goodwill and momentum that can help propel the parties through the more difficult negotiations; others say you're better off tackling major issues first, especially if failing to reach agreement on the major issue would make the minor issues moot.

Step 3: Expressing Disagreement and Conflict

Disagreement and conflict are commonplace in negotiations. If you're wise, you'll learn from these; they reveal something about the interests of the other side. Consequently, you should expect and welcome this phase of negotiations. Handling conflict effectively will bring the parties together; handling it poorly will divide them.

When presenting issues, most negotiators will tell you what they "want." It is your job to find out what they "need" or will settle for. Few negotiators get everything they want. It might be in your best interest to occasionally compromise or modify your goals as you learn more. In fact, it's best to remain flexible throughout the negotiating process.

Don't view conflict as a test of power but as a chance to find out what people need.

Step 4: Reassessing and Compromising

At some point in difficult negotiations, one party may signal its willingness to compromise. If you hear statements that begin with "Suppose that . . . ?" or "What if . . . ?" or "How would you feel about . . . ?" listen closely; the other side may be hinting at a move closer to your position. Don't try to pin the other side down quickly, because this could cause him or her to withdraw. Instead, play along. Say, "Well, there are several possibilities."

When responding to statements of goals, positions, and offers, it's a good idea to use the reflective listening technique described earlier. If the other side offers to sell you a car for $22,000, you should say, "So you're offering this auto to me for $22,000?" If you use this technique:

- The other side may improve the offer because he thinks your response is a negative.

- The other side may try to justify his position. This will provide you with opportunities to challenge his assumptions.

- You will gain time to think about a counteroffer. If the other side repeats your counteroffer, confirm it; don't sweeten it. This forces the other side to accept it, reject it, or suggest an alternative.

Step 5: Reaching Agreement

At this stage you settle on an agreement—ideally *in writing*. Volunteer to do the contract writing. This gives you tremendous power. As you go along in the negotiations, take written notes on all small agreements. And make sure that they find their way into the final agreement. "So, if I agree to buy the house, you'll repair the back-yard fence and remove the old oil tank from the cellar before the closing, is that right?" Then visibly write it down. Let the other side know you're keeping track of those small agreements. You can even provide copies of all the small agreements you both have made during negotiations.

Make sure you have an agreement that gives everyone an incentive to comply with its terms. There should be negative consequences for noncompliance, for example, a financial penalty for not delivering materials on time. Document the agreement and obtain sign-offs by decision makers. Then stay in touch with the other party while the agreement is implemented.

TACTICS

Now that you understand the five steps that most negotiations go through, let's consider some practical tactics you can employ to come out with the deal you want. There's nothing mysterious about these, and they are not by any means the only negotiating tactics available. But taken together they can give you a big advantage. These tactics are:

- Framing the issue
- Setting an anchor price
- Offering alternative deals
- Using time to advantage
- Closing the deal

Framing the Issue

People operate with mental frameworks that shape perceived reality. Their framework is the lens through which they see things. For example, in describing the state of the nation, an economist will assess the state of the union in terms of annual domestic product, per capita income, the unemployment rate, and similar values. That's the economist's frame. A sociologist, in contrast, would talk about trends in class stratification, family stability, demographic trends, and the number of people in the criminal justice system. Because of their training and interests, economists and sociologists frame reality in very different ways.

As a negotiator, you can gain advantage if you can get the other side to adopt your framing of the issues at hand. For example, if you are negotiating wages with shop employees, you might frame the situation in terms of *how well you are currently paying them* relative to what local competitors are paying their shop employees.

> "Yes, we are agreeable to some wage adjustments for the coming year, but you have to recognize that your average wage and benefits are $18.50 per hour—that's already 15 percent above what Acme Assembly and Jones Industries, our two local competitors, are paying their people to do essentially the same work."

Of course, if he is on the ball, the leader of the shop workers will try to shrug off that frame and impose one that is more favorable to him, such as productivity:

> "Yes, Acme and Jones are paying less, but they are also getting less in return than we give to this company. While Acme and Jones are just breaking even, this company has become more profitable in each of the past four years—in large part because of employee productivity. Just look at your per-unit cost of assembly!"

Whoever successfully frames the issues will have a leg up in the negotiations that follow. That's because the other side is negotiating on the framer's terms. Here's another example:

Sheila is a project manager in charge of developing and install-ing a new corporate e-commerce Web site. She wants senior management to increase the project's budget from $500,000 to $650,000 to accommodate unanticipated changes. Knowing that management will argue against her request strictly on fi-nancial terms, she frames her request in nonfinancial terms: how her plan will improve the performance of the system and of the organization as a whole:

"As our team has gathered input from each of the product groups, we've learned about their needs, and what it will take to make the system more adaptable to product and pricing changes, and to make the customer experience better. This will, of course, cost more, but will improve Web site perfor-mance by at least 25 percent."

In this case, Sheila has tried to reframe the issue from money to something that is of equal importance to management: perfor-mance. If her framing is successful, discussion will center not on the added cost of the Web site, but on how changes could make it more useful to the product groups and to customers—a potential win-win.

Think for a moment about the last negotiation in which you were involved. How was the key issue framed?

Did you frame the key issue, or did the other side? _____

Setting an Anchor Price

In the jargon of negotiating, an *anchor* is a psychological reference point for subsequent discussion. For example, when you go look-ing for a house to purchase, the listing agent will have already dropped an anchor: "The Perfect Condo in a Prestigious Neighbor-hood—and Only $395,000." For most buyers, that price becomes the reference point for negotiation with the seller. The buyer will want to offer less, but not by an order of magnitude. For example, in this case the prospective buyer might offer $350,000, expecting a counteroffer somewhere below the listing price—say, $385,000.

An anchor is useful for whoever sets it in that it creates a perception of possible outcomes. If the anchor holds, the deal will be negotiated somewhere near the anchor price. Thus, the party that sets the anchor in an area favorable to her gains an important advantage.

Where should you place the anchor? If you are a seller, and if you have some notion of the buyer's reserve price (the maximum the buyer will pay), try dropping your anchor just below that price. Then be prepared to justify that price when the potential buyer tries to talk you down. Recognize, however, that your ability to set the anchor will be limited by competitive force. For example, in the "Perfect Condo" example, the price must generally reflect what similar condos in the city or neighborhood are selling for. An outrageously high price would be ridiculed.

If the other party has already set the anchor price—one that you view as wide of the mark—try to "counteranchor." For example, if you were a potential buyer in the condo example, you might say something like this:

> "I respect your wish to get the most for your condo, which is a very nice property. You have every reason to be proud of it. However, based on my analysis of it and comparable properties, I believe that $395,000 overstates its true market value. My study of comparable condos in this area, considering square footage and amenities, indicates that $330,000 is closer to its true value. If you are willing to entertain that price, I'd be glad to discuss the sale with you."

If you've done homework that supports that lower price—and assuming that $330,000 is above the seller's reserve price (the lowest she'll take for her condo)—there's a good chance that your counteranchor will hold. Bargaining will then take place around that point.

. . . .

TIP: BACK UP YOUR ANCHOR WITH FACTS.

If you want your anchor—or counteranchor—to hold, be prepared to justify it. For instance, in the condo counteranchor example you might bring along the analysis you've done of comparable condo properties and prices.

. . . .

Think about your next negotiating experience. How could employing a price anchor work to your advantage?

_____

_____

What steps would you take to counter if the other side has already placed an anchor?

_____

_____

Using Time to Advantage

Time is a valuable commodity and no less so in the business of negotiating. If you are a seller with no compelling reason to sell right away, time is your ally. For example, Helen has listed her dry cleaning business for sale for $650,000. But since she doesn't need the money at the moment—and she's not planning to retire soon— she's in no big rush. Time is on her side. "If I don't get a buyer at that price," she tells her family, "I'll just continue operating the business, which pays me a good income. And the business becomes more valuable over time."

But time can be your enemy. For example, John has listed his house for sale at $350,000. Time is not on his side, as he signed a noncontingent agreement to purchase a new house four months from now. And he needs the cash from the sale of the first house to make good on his agreement to buy the second. Otherwise, he must obtain an expensive bridge loan.

Helen and John are in very different places with respect to time. Free of time pressure, Helen can reject offers below her asking price. "I'll just wait for a better offer to come along," she says. John, however, is in a tight spot. His bargaining position weakens with every passing week.

The lesson in the stories of Helen and John is that you should think about time as you enter any negotiation. Is it on your side or working against you? You can also use time as a bargaining tool. Here's one example, using John and his for-sale house as a prop:

> Samantha has her eye on John's house. She likes the house, its features, and its location. She also knows through a friend about John's commitment to purchase a new house. Thus, she knows that John is in a time bind. So she makes this offer: "I'll agree to purchase your house for $295,000. But that offer will expire in exactly five business days." John is now in the hot seat. He has an offer that is lower than he'd hoped for, but it's an offer from a qualified buyer, and the *only* offer he has at the moment. And unless he can find a better offer within five days (highly unlikely), this offer will disappear. Should he take it or wait for something better? Meanwhile, the clock is ticking.

In effect, Samantha has offered to trade something that John needs (a timely purchase) for something that she wants (a lower price) using time as a lever.

Time has an impact on the progress of negotiations and the willingness of parties to make concessions. Even if you don't know the time constraints on the other side, you can surmise them by looking for the following clues:

■ They pick up the pace of discussion.

■ They suddenly soften an earlier hard-line position.

■ They become preoccupied with how much time has passed (e.g., a lot of glancing at watches).

■ A new person (e.g., a higher-level executive) suddenly enters the negotiation.

■ They concede an issue.

When it serves your purposes, you can create time pressure on the other side to move discussion along or to resolve a deadlock. Try:

■ Letting the other side think that your supply of what she wants is limited (e.g., "We have only three of these pickup trucks in stock and they're going fast")

■ Referring to an imminent price increase

■ Making a limited-time offer (as described earlier)

■ Making an offer contingent on an immediate response

Be wary, however, of creating a false deadline. A skilled opponent will call your bluff by ignoring it. Once the deadline passes, you'll lose your credibility.

· ·

TIP: WITHHOLD AS MANY CONCESSIONS AS POSSIBLE UNTIL THE END.

Eighty percent of concessions tend to be made during the last 20 percent of the negotiating session. A concession that means little to the other side in the early going may be just the thing to close the deal.

· ·

What time constraints do you face?

How will you hide your time deadlines?

_____

Are there any timing considerations that could help you make a better deal?

_____

Offering Alternative Deals

Not every potential resolution must take the form of a single offer like this: "We are prepared to offer you $550,000 for your dry cleaning establishment." Instead, smart deals often take the form of package alternatives. That way, if the other side is dissatisfied with one aspect of the package, say, the price, he or she may be attracted to some other part of the package.

> "Here's what we propose, Helen. We can pay you $550,000 for ownership of the dry cleaning business, and we are willing to close on that deal anytime over the next four months at your convenience. Further, we can offer you half-time employment at $3,000 per month for the 12 months following the sale. That will provide income for you and keep the business on an even keel as we learn to run it. Finally, as an incentive for you to help us through the transition, we are prepared to give you 5 percent of net profits above the $40,000 mark for the first two years after the sale. That way, if we win, you win."

Multioption deals such as this one provide plenty of win-win opportunities. In this example, the timing of the sale, the part-time employment of the current owner in the postclose business, and a reward for healthy profits each represent a potential win-win.

Other occasions for deal alternatives are available when the value at stake can be partitioned in some way. Consider this example:

Bill owns a small breakfast and lunch café in a high-traffic strip mall. Joanne, who owns the space adjacent to the café, would like to buy and expand her popular sporting goods shop into Bill's space. But what would she do with all the cooking equipment, tables, chairs, and so forth? She'd have to sell them at auction when they might be more valuable to Bill.

Joanne makes this proposal to Bill: "I'll buy your place as is for $400,000. Alternatively, I'll give you $350,000 for the space and let you keep all the fixtures."

The second option might be more attractive to Bill if he wants to open a new café in another location. He'd have all the fixtures and equipment needed to go into business. It would also save Joanne the time and trouble of unloading those items, which are of no use to her. In cases like this, knowing your interests and the interests of the other side will help you find options that benefit both parties.

. . . .

Can you think of ways you might partition the offer you are now negotiating? How would these alternative options create more value for you and for the other side?

_____

_____

_____

Closing the Deal

Assuming that you hit no deal-breaking impediments, you'll eventually get to the point of closing your negotiations. That conclusion will be more successful if you do a few things:

■ **Don't allow the other side to reopen issues that have already been settled.** For example, if you've already agreed on the price, the timing of the sale, and other terms, don't allow the other side to reopen any of those issues as you draft the final document. This is why it's a good idea to write down agreements on issues *as they are resolved.* If the other side insists on reopening one issue, take that as your right to reopen *all* issues to negotiation. Neither party should have the right to pick and choose. "If you weren't happy with the price, you should have said so earlier, before we agreed on that point. But if you insist on renegotiating the price, then that will affect the terms and timing of the sale from our perspective since we see these as a total package. Is that what you want?"

■ **Make it official.** Either a verbal restatement of the agreement, a handshake, or a meticulous formal contract is in order, depending on the situation. But written agreements are always best. Even deals between family members benefit from written agreements.

■ **Include enforcement mechanisms.** Many negotiations involve promises. "I'll do this if you'll do that." But what if someone fails to make good on his promises? Your agreement should spell out the consequences: "If interest and principal is not paid as scheduled, the entire outstanding balance of the loan will be due."

CHAPTER REVIEW

To discover what you have learned so far, take the following open-book review quiz.

1. Describe the five basic steps of negotiating.

_____

_____

_____

2. Why is framing the issues so important?

_____

_____

_____

3. What is an anchor price and how does it influence subsequent negotiations?

_____

_____

_____

4. Give one example of how a negotiator can use time to his or her advantage.

_____

_____

_____

CHAPTER 9

COMMON PITFALLS

S ounds pretty easy so far, doesn't it? The steps and tactics described in the previous chapters can take you a long way. But watch out: There are some crafty players out there and you don't want to run afoul of their negotiating ploys. We'll cover some of those ploys here. We'll also identify common errors you must avoid, what to do when negotiations fail, and some things that American readers should keep in mind as they negotiate across national and cultural borders.

NEGOTIATING PLOYS

Although win-win negotiations are becoming the norm, you're still going to run into folks who have succeeded through old-school hard bargaining. Their aim is to create win-lose outcomes that favor them. Here, you need to remember the story about the guy with lots of money who encountered someone else who had plenty of experience. In that story, the guy who once had all the money ended up with "an experience" and the other fellow ended up with

the money. Your best defense against such people is to know the
ploys they'll use and how to counteract them.

The Hardball Bargainer

Hardball bargainers take an unreasonable opening position,
hoping to force you to lower your expectations. An unprepared
negotiator will panic and make early concessions. If you are prepared—you know your best alternative to negotiating and your reserve price—you will be less easily intimidated.

When faced with an extreme demand, restate it in your own
words in terms more acceptable to you. Don't counter with your
own list of unreasonable demands. You should, however, ask for
more than you expect. This will give you some negotiating room. If
you start off with a bottom offer, you'll have no more room to ma-
neuver. How much more should you ask for? Try bracketing. If you
want to pay no more than $75,000 for a piece of production equip-
ment and the seller asks for $80,000, try offering $70,000. Leave
room for negotiating a win-win agreement.

If the other side is annoyingly overbearing, unyielding, and
clearly trying to take advantage of you, give that person a quizzical
look, as if to say (but without stating it), "Are we dealing with a
fool?" Then firmly but politely say something like this: "We have
no interest in that arrangement. Is that your offer?" The other side
must either then begin acting reasonable or risk losing the whole
deal.

Take It or Leave It

One tactic designed to undercut your feeling of power and to lower
your expectations is the "take it or leave it" ploy. In this case, restate your position and its benefits to the other side. Let the other
side know that their offer is unworkable and unacceptable as it
stands—and that you *will* leave it. As a means of self-encourage-
ment, remind yourself that the other side has an interest in making
a deal. Why else would they be talking to you? Your "leaving it" will

cost them. If you've gained insights into their best alternative to a deal, you may know that walking away is not a good option for them.

Never tolerate a temper tantrum.

The Temper Tantrum

If the other side throws a temper tantrum, be very clear that that behavior will not be tolerated. Stand up and say something like this: "We cannot continue these negotiations until you have re-gained your composure. Our group will adjourn to the cafeteria for some coffee while you do that. Let us know when and *if* we can reconvene." If the same behavior is repeated once you reconvene, walk out.

The Salami Slice

The practitioner of the "salami slice" tactic takes a little of what he wants every so often until he ends up with the lion's share of the value. The origin of this strategy is attributed to Matyas Rakosis, the general secretary of the Hungarian Communist Party, who ex-plained that when you want to get hold of a salami that opponents are defending, you must not grab at it. Instead, you should carve a very thin slice for yourself. The salami's owner will either not notice it, or not mind very much. The next day, you carve another slice, then another until, little by little, you will have the entire salami.

A little here, a little there, and pretty soon you have nothing left. That's the salami slice ploy. Counter it by following the advice given in the previous chapter: Write down agreements as they are made. If you do this, you'll easily notice how much of the value is being sliced off by the other side.

The Good Guy–Bad Guy Routine

This ploy involves the other side bringing in a person you haven't seen before—the bad guy—who tears your offer to pieces, makes unreasonable demands, and storms out of the room. Then the original negotiator, the good guy, makes what seem to be reasonable requests—reasonable, that is, relative to what the bad guy offered. Their plan is to get you to make concessions that the good guy can sell to the bad guy. The way you counter this is to recognize that everyone on the other side is a "bad" guy. Ask for a recess, review your original plan, affirm its goals among your team members, and resume negotiations.

It's Standard Practice

The other side might also try a "standard practice" or "standard contract" ploy. This is a common ploy when one side (yours) has no experience in a particular industry while the other has plenty. The common medium for this ploy is to offer the other side a printed contract, most terms of which are favorable to whichever side drew it up. For instance, in the book-publishing industry, the standard contract allows the author to purchase copies of her own work under terms that are far less generous than those offered to resellers, such as bookstores. It's a safe bet that the novice author will not be familiar with the industry's terms of trade and may actually think that she is getting a good deal. If the author should ask about those terms, "Oh, this is a standard contract" will be the reply. The assumption is that no one would want to change the contract because it is "standard."

Just remember two things if you encounter this ploy: First, standard practices and standard contracts will almost always disadvantage you to the benefit of the other side. Second, everything is potentially negotiable; parties can put anything into a contract that is not against the law or public policy.

The Last-Minute Grab

The last-minute grab (or nibble) is an attempt to get a concession near the end of negotiations when you are tired, frustrated, and probably want to go home—when you are least likely to walk away from the table. The artful practitioner of this ploy will watch you and the clock. She may sense your eagerness to wrap things up so that you can leave. She may know, for instance, that you have a 6 P.M. flight home tonight, and that you will miss that flight and have to spend another night in a local hotel if everything cannot be negotiated within the next half hour. It is during those waning minutes that the last-minute grabber will ask for concessions. "If we can just settle this one thing, we should be able to wrap this up and get you on your way."

There are two defenses against the last-minute grab. The first is to keep track of the time and the number of unsettled issues that remain as time passes. The second is to make a mental calculation of the cost of the concession relative to the cost of an extra hotel night and a missed flight. Corporate businesspeople are not always good at this second defense. A missed night at home costs them personally; the concession they make is borne by someone else: shareholders they have probably never met.

Can you think of other ploys your opponent might use? How could you counter them?

COMMON MISTAKES

Good tactics and knowing how to cope with the other side's ploys will take you far as a negotiator. But be wary of tripping yourself up. Like tennis players, many negotiators lose games through their own mistakes. Research has found that the following are the most common kinds of mistakes negotiators make:

■ **Being inadequately prepared.** Like anything else in life, you have to be prepared. Do you know what you want and need? Do you know what you can give up? Do you know the same about your opponent? Do you know your best alternative to a deal with the other side, and the price or conditions under which you would be better off by walking away?

■ **Trying to win at any cost.** This kind of error is fed by a number of psychological factors, including the ego of the negotiator and his or her compulsive competitive instinct. The result may be a lose-lose deal and a broken relationship with the other side. Commitment to a course of action, no matter what, often biases perception and judgment. The win-at-any-cost bargainer will look for evidence to support his viewpoint and ignore information to the contrary. Research shows that the tougher the tactics, the tougher the resistance. Persuasion, not dominance, makes for a better outcome.

A related error is called *irrational escalation.* Desperate to win (or avoid the humiliation of defeat), the negotiator will raise the stakes beyond the point where they make sense. This phenomenon is frequently seen in auctions and in hostile takeover gambits. Auctions are by nature competitive, and competitive people want to win, even if they pay too much. In the case of hostile takeovers and similar business transactions, CEOs with inflated egos will escalate their bids for acquisition targets far above the intrinsic value of those enterprises. And since few subordinates have the stomach for getting between their boss's big ego and the object of his or her fixation, no one will say, "Boss, you're acting goofy." Irrational escalation may be one of the reasons that 70 percent of mergers and acquisitions fail to deliver on buyer expectations—someone paid too much!

Watch out for the boss's big ego.

A practical way to check the win-at-any-cost/escalation error is to agree—as a team—to the following: "We will go this far and no further; beyond that point, this deal makes no sense."

■ **Failing to properly "frame" the situation.** As described in the previous chapter, proper framing of the issue or issues can make a major difference in the outcome. So state your position in positive terms. For example, tell the other side, "Our wage proposal of $12 an hour is $2 more than you are now receiving," rather than, "I know you wanted $15 an hour, but $12 an hour is the best I can do." A negative slant can cause the other side to make fewer concessions and may lead to an impasse.

■ **Being overconfident.** This psychological trap causes negotiators to inflate their perception of their own power and to underestimate their opponents. Overconfidence encourages negotiators to (1) not challenge their own beliefs and assumptions, and (2) disregard information that contradicts what they believe. Within organizations, overconfidence takes the form of *groupthink*, a condition in which opinions converge into a singular viewpoint and from which dissenting views are suppressed. One effective antidote to overconfidence and groupthink is to have one respected and powerful member of your team challenge prevailing assumptions and point out weaknesses in your position.

How many of these mistakes have you made? Fortunately, because they are self-inflicted, it is within the power of every negotiator to avoid them.

> There are two other ways to settle really difficult disputes: *arbitration* and *mediation.*

. . . .

WHEN NEGOTIATION FAILS

Sometimes it isn't possible to negotiate a satisfactory outcome. There may be a fundamental disagreement over the facts, assumptions, price, or other critical issues. Don't give up. Aside from just walking away there are two other ways to settle really difficult disputes: *arbitration* and *mediation.*

Arbitration is the use of an impartial third party to hear both sides of a dispute and to render a decision, which is usually binding. It may be helpful when both sides can't or won't budge from their positions.

Mediation is the attempt by an impartial third party to help the two sides in a dispute to communicate, negotiate, and reach agreement. Unlike an arbitrator, the mediator is a facilitator; he or she does not decide the outcome. Mediation is usually voluntary and nonbinding.

. . . .

NEGOTIATING INTERNATIONALLY

If you are an American reader, you should understand that the negotiating skills and techniques used successfully at home may not work as well abroad. That's important in an era of growing global travel and business. This section will provide you with a few tips on how to be more successful when dealing across national borders.

One of the keys to successful international negotiating is an awareness of how people from other cultures perceive you. The minute you walk into a room full of people from another culture, you are stereotyped. Whether the stereotype is right or wrong is beside the point. It happens, and you have to be aware of it because other people's perception of you affects negotiations; so does your perception of them. It's therefore a good idea to know how Americans are often seen by their counterparts in other countries.

Probably the best piece of advice for dealing with people from other cultures is to try to surprise them by confounding their stereotype of you. Most non-Americans see Americans as geographically and culturally illiterate, and with good reason. So before you meet your counterparts, learn something about their country, region, business culture, and language. Pull out an atlas. Look up your counterparts' country and study it. Read about the region. What economic and political issues dominate the news there? Armed with that rudimentary knowledge, you can ask intelligent questions about their homeland.

In addition, most non-English speakers think (rightly) that Americans know only English. Surprise them by learning a few words of their language. Start with pleasantries such as *I'm very pleased to meet you, hello, goodbye,* and *how are you?* You don't have to be fluent (although fluency would help); just making the effort will pay goodwill dividends.

Frank Acuff, in his book, *How to Negotiate Anything with Anyone Anywhere Around the World,* identified a number of traits that characterize American negotiators and analyzed the impact of those traits on cross-border negotiations:

■ **Americans are seen as direct communicators.** To many people, this trait may translate as being pushy and offensively blunt. Such behavior is not common in many Latin American and Asian cultures. By being blunt, you risk missing the little things that the other side is communicating. For example, only rarely do Mexicans and Japanese answer yes or no. When the Japanese say yes they mean only that they have heard you. When they say, "That will be difficult," they mean no. You have to judge the response in the context of what is being communicated, not what is actually said. Many Europeans, too, don't allow emotions or relationships to run their negotiations. Germans especially can be as deal oriented as Americans. As a general rule, Europeans are a bit more formal than Americans in business relationships. For example, the English tend not to appreciate personal questions, and Germans put great emphasis on titles, preferring to be called Herr Professor Shultz, rather than Helmut. When in doubt, *ask.* "What would you like me to call you?" isn't a bad opening question. Better to err on the side of formality.

■ **Americans are impatient and seem rushed.** This kind of behavior can lead to unnecessary concessions by Americans to the other side, who may be *very* patient. So, *slow down* when negotiating internationally. Put yourself in the time frame of the other side's culture. Being in the same time frame is another way of being on the same wavelength.

■ **Americans normally negotiate alone rather than in teams.** People from other cultures may think that a lone American doesn't take the negotiations seriously and isn't very well prepared.

Americans are often seen as "lone cowboys" who want to do it all and in a hurry. To remedy this, work within a team. Break up the workload. You're at a disadvantage if you let one person try to handle the entire negotiations, because the other side will be working as a team.

■ **Americans tend to emphasize the short term, the immediate deal, instead of the long-term relationship.** This transactional behavior probably comes from Americans' "quarterly report" mind-set, whereas their foreign counterparts are likely to be compensated for results achieved over a period of years, not months. Asians, in particular, tend to value relationships. They trust the person with whom they are negotiating, rather than a contract, and see the agreement as the starting point, not the final solution. In some Asian countries, a signed contract can be invalidated if circumstances change. To succeed in international negotiations, look for the long-term payoff and prove your commitment to the other side by your language and actions.

■ **Americans emphasize content over relationships.** The typical American, after exchanging pleasantries, wants to get down to business. Americans are also logical, factual, and legalistic. Americans tend to prefer lengthy written contracts, which makes others believe that Americans don't trust themselves or others. Negotiators from the Middle East, Latin America, and many Asian countries, for example, see this as an affront to friendship and trust. Again, slow down, listen, and get to know your counterpart at a personal level before you begin negotiating. Also, if you need something in writing, make it short and conversational. No court has ever thrown out a contract because it was too easy to understand.

An American negotiator who hopes to succeed in international negotiations has to be flexible and must approach people of other cultures from their point of view. Others may expect you to act in what they see as negative American ways. If you pleasantly surprise them, the goodwill you generate will serve your cause well throughout the negotiating process.

CHAPTER REVIEW

To review what you have learned, take the following open-book review quiz.

1. Your counterpart is throwing a temper tantrum. Describe options for dealing with this.

   _____

   _____

2. Describe at least three other negotiating ploys listed in the chapter. How could you effectively respond to these?

   _____

   _____

   _____

3. Explain the self-inflicted error called irrational escalation. Can you give an example of it?

   _____

   _____

4. Name two ways to settle disputes or impasses when negotiations fail.

   _____

   _____

5. Imagine that you will be traveling to Madrid to negotiate a product distribution agreement with a Spanish company. Outside of the substantive business issues, how would you prepare for your meeting? How would you approach your interactions with the Spanish company's negotiating team?

   _____

   _____

SELECTED READINGS

Acuff, Frank. *How to Negotiate Anything with Anyone Anywhere Around the World.* New York: AMACOM Books, 1993.

Bazerman, Max H., and Margaret A. Neale. *Negotiating Rationally.* New York: Free Press, 1992.

Fisher, Roger, William Ury, and Bruce Patton. *Getting to Yes: Negotiating Agreement Without Giving In,* 2nd ed. New York: Penguin, 1991.

Sebenius, James. "Six Habits of Merely Effective Negotiators." *Harvard Business Review,* April, 2001.

Volkema, Roger. *Leverage.* New York: AMACOM Books, 2005.

Watkins, Michael. *Breakthrough Negotiations.* New York: John Wiley & Sons, 2002.

INDEX

Announcing!